Praise For

A Shepherdess Beaten But Never Broken

"Reading this book was a gift of inspiration motivated by vulnerability, courage, tenacity and strength. The emotional rollercoaster of the highs and the lows, and ability to connect as a reader to Deb's story was unmatched leaving me wanting to read more about someone who has been an inspiration for so many to keep pushing forward no matter what challenges one encounters, and to remain humble."

Adam Motyczka, Licensed Clinical Social Worker–Florida

"To say I was pleased and surprised at the contents of this book and the story it told are an understatement. To tell a personal story is hard in itself, but to do so with such ease and the description of the emotions that are being felt with so much clarity is unique. Keeping my interest from beginning to end, as I read the book it was easy to imagine being there with the author during her life's journey. After reading the book I have a clearer understanding of the love the author had for life, and by writing this book to help others understand their journey through life as well. A job well done."

Ollie Smith, President & CEO Horizon Health–Illinois

"As I read through each page, I was able to create my own images of her story as I went through a battery of emotions. In this book you will discover what true darkness is like, you will feel the helplessness of a young child.

In the middle of all the darkness there was hope and light and the love of the animals she cared for and the love they had for her. This book shows what it is like being knocked down but the true inspiration for me was how she was able to rise again time after time. She never comprised her standards in life.

This is truly an amazing story with several surprises and twists through her incredible life from humble beginnings to incredible personal and professional achievements. She is a true shepherdess leading us all through her incredible journey one page at a time. It is my profound honor to recommend this book to those who are ready to be inspired."

Cliff Macke, Director of Sales The Prairie Press–Illinois

"The book was so intriguing that I didn't want to put it down. I read it in a day and a half, and it made me want more. A true story of a little girl and her determination to be who she is today! A must read."

Deb Bell, Belmar Farms–Ohio

"An incredible story of strength, determination and an undying light. Shine on Deb, shine on. This true story is an inspiration and an eye-opener to what one can achieve even when it seems the darkest."

Douglas Lancaster, Indiana

"I have a lot of respect for Deb because of her accomplishments as a stockperson and her ability to evaluate and breed high-quality sheep–but I can honestly say that I didn't really know her until I read her story. This is a rollercoaster of a life story, documenting the resilient capacity of the American woman and a Shepherdess that is tough to beat".

Scott A. Bowdridge, Ph.D., Professor of Food Animal Production
Davis College–West Virginia

A SHEPHERDESS BEATEN

BUT NEVER BROKEN

A True Story of Resilience, Triumph, and
Overcoming Adversity with Grace

A SHEPHERDESS
BEATEN
BUT NEVER BROKEN

A True Story of Resilience, Triumph, and
Overcoming Adversity with Grace

DEBBY JO HOLMQUIST

Published by Victorious You Press™
Charlotte NC, USA

TITLE: A SHEPHERDESS BEATEN BUT NEVER BROKEN
First Printed: 2025
Cover Designer: Nadia Monsano – Elite Creations
Editor: Charmaine Castillo

ISBN: 978-1-959719-41-0
ISBN: (eBook) 978-1-959719-42-7
Library of Congress Control Number: 2024921425

Printed in the United States of America

For details email joan@victoriousyoupress.com
or visit us at www.victoriousyoupress.com

DEDICATION

This book is dedicated to those who have loved and believed in me. I will treasure your kindness forever. To the ones reading this who may have endured abuse, neglect, and made to feel powerless, I hope this story will inspire you to never doubt yourself and the dream that dwells in your soul. It is yours and no one else's. Do not let it falter; go after it with all your might.

Your journey will provide you with courage and strength to overcome doubts, fears, challenges, and obstacles. The gift of your dream will become priceless and will reward you in ways you cannot imagine. Do not settle for the ordinary.

Your dreams await you. NEVER GIVE UP!

ACKNOWLEDGEMENTS

I would like to express my deepest gratitude to my long-time dear friend and writing coach, Leslie Cottrell, for her unwavering encouragement, patience, grace, and expertise in mentoring me through the journey of writing my story. I could not have undertaken this without you. God sent you to me. To my editor, Charmaine Roots Castillo, my heartfelt thanks for your magnificent talent, dedication, and hard work on my story. You are the wind beneath the wings of this book.

Special thanks to Joan T. Randall of Victorious You Press for your wonderful support, expert guidance and patience in bringing my story to life!

To my treasured friends Andrea (Lovey); Mallory (Bob); and Ruth-Ann, for your loving support and opinions and your time spent on reviewing and assisting me with my drafts. You light up this world. To my Maine neighbors, Pam and Louise, for always being there for me with an open heart. I consider it a privilege to call you my friends.

To Bruce, for encouraging me years ago to write my story and share it with others who may benefit from it. I am forever grateful for your love and belief in me along with your endless support in all ways.

To my forever family, Juston, Hannah and Emma Rae, I love you endlessly.

TABLE OF CONTENTS

FOREWORD

The story you are about to read is an incredible true recapitulation of a most remarkable life. It details an abusive childhood experience that would be considered criminal by today's standards. The story expounds on an escape from a very dark world and then doing what it takes to survive. What follows is a remarkable journey into the competitive world of producing championship purebred Dorset sheep, and how this amazing female, on a shoestring budget, competed against multimillion-aires winning multiple national championships! The overwhelming amount of stress she had to endure to achieve her goals should be inspirational to all who read her story. This is the type of book one cannot put down once started. It describes a life experience of extreme cruelty and amazing successes. It will touch your emotions and cause you to ponder your own lives and inspire you to follow your dreams. It has been my honor to have known this remarkable lady and a privilege to write this foreword to her true-life story.

YOU are about to embark on an amazing trip; one of cruelty, survival, extreme hardships, humor, and wonderful successes. It is a true story written in the author's own words that will touch your emotions and yet inspire you.

Dr. Bruce J. Houle

INTRODUCTION

In 1996, I stood in the show arena of the most renowned Dorset sheep show and sale in the nation, "The Ohio Dorset Show and Sale." Countless spectators filled the bleachers, leaving standing room only in every direction. Farmers from all over the country attended the exhibition and subsequent auction of the finest sheep.

The sale generated a substantial income for the breeders who consigned their animals. It also provided an opportunity for other sheep breeders to purchase superior genetics to enhance their breeding programs. Standing beside my sheep, ready to line up for the auction, I heard the announcement that the sale would begin in five minutes. The competition featured top-notch sheep presented by experienced exhibitors from the United States and Canada. A points system was used to determine the recipient of the most distinguished award among breeders. Winning a class or consistently placing high in the competition was how breeders achieved victory. The highest achievement a sheep breeder could receive at a show and sale was the coveted "Best Consignment Award." When the sale manager was ready to announce the winner, my jumbled emotions of excitement and nerves had reached their peak. Silence dropped over the crowd in anticipation, and I heard these words:

"This year's winner is Sugarloaf Dorsets from Maine! Debby Jo, will you please step up onto the auction block to receive this award?"

With the sound of thunderous applause in my ears, all I could see was the flash of cameras. I gripped the solid, ornately crafted 8 x 10 walnut plaque and was rooted in that present moment. My eyes gazed down at the plaque and read the gold-plated inscription: "1996 National Dorset Show and Sale – Best Consignment Award." I was fully aware that I was living the best day of my entire life. I struggled to keep my tears at bay while observing the crowd's joyful and supportive presence. The road I had traveled was marked by challenges that no one else knew about. This moment captured my heart, stirring feelings of pride and emotion within me.

From an early age, my dream had been to participate in the very arena where I had just won the coveted prize. I remained steadfast in aiming for the stars, despite the years of negative whispers behind my back. I was standing in the moment of achieving what I once thought was an unattainable goal. I achieved it--against all odds.

For years I thought about and dreamed about how it might feel to be on top, and that day, in that moment, surrounded by pats on the back, handshakes, and embraces, I was captivated. In the midst of that celebration, I caught a glimpse of a memory from twenty years earlier of my father spitting in my face, shouting, "You will never be anything, or ever raise a sheep without my help!" That was the day I left my family home, carrying just half a bag of clothes and eight dollars in pennies.

I have a story to share about a young girl with blonde hair and pigtails, who was well aware of her life's aspirations. She aimed to become a professional shepherd. Despite the challenges, she stayed true to herself, did the work, and remained focused. Staying positive helped her achieve her goal. She sacrificed years of her life doing something she was not enthusiastic about to pursue what she genuinely loved. That girl was me, and this is my story of triumph. Despite enduring years of incomprehensible cruelty, abuse, injustice, heartbreak, disappointment, and struggle, I used grit, faith, hope, and resilience to achieve my dream by never giving up.

Along the way, I experienced incredible moments and met treasured people. Throughout my journey, I have gained valuable lessons that will inspire others to believe in themselves even when others do not.

Remember, you are enough. Your life and dreams are your own, not anyone else's. If it is in your heart, it is meant to be.

"Never underestimate the heart of a champion."

—Coach Rudy Tomjanovich

CHAPTER ONE
Facing Adversity

I was left alone at the old farmhouse we lived in for hours at a time. I was not old enough to attend school yet, so I spent day in and day out fending for myself. I wandered out to the barn to play with the barn kittens and sat amongst the sheep in an old wooden octagon-shaped hay crib keeping myself occupied. I was extremely lonely and found myself always longing for someone to spend time with me.

Toys and books were scarce, so I learned to entertain myself. I explored the farm pastures, following the sheep on their hoof-beaten paths, and took exploratory journeys through the thick forest surrounding the farm. My creativity and imagination were my constant companions, helping me create my own toys from items I found around the farm. I scavenged my father's workshop and found piles of scrap wood, old barrels full of rusty nails, nuts, and bolts, and an assortment of old faucet handles and pipe fittings. I spent hours constructing several handmade wooden sailboats, nailing pieces together and using pieces of string cut off from the bales of hay. I found outdated cans of paint in assorted colors, and used that to paint my sail boats before launching them in the farm pond to see how far they could sail.

I dedicated my days to improving my construction abilities, building a tiny playhouse in the woods, complete with fastening boards to trees to mimic kitchen shelves. Mixing water and dirt in an old bucket, I made mud pies to stack on the shelves. I decorated my mud cakes with pinecones and spruce tree twigs to make them more enticing, and pretended that someone might come by to purchase my works of art.

When I entered the first grade at the age of seven, I was lacking the basic skills that attendance in preschool or kindergarten would have prepared me for. My first teacher, Mrs. Kinnear, was a very kind, frail, gray-haired lady who started us out by teaching us how to count pennies. I remember her holding the copper coins in her hands as she gently and kindly shared her knowledge with us. Mrs. Kinnear gave me a package of flashcards to take home so I could get some extra help and catch up with the rest of the class. I was excited to learn new skills and couldn't wait to get home to start practicing. When I got home, I presented my pack of flashcards to my mother and quietly asked if she would help me learn them.

"Get upstairs and learn them yourself!" she snorted, not even turning her head to make eye contact. A wave of sadness and rejection came over me as I slipped out of her sight. My mother never showed any interest in my school progress. I continued to struggle in school, and when it was time to bring home my progress report, I learned that report card day was synonymous with torture day.

My father was a heavy-boned man who stood over six feet tall and weighed over three hundred pounds. He was powerful and strong with huge, hard and weathered bony hands. His dark piercing eyes and scornful expression were the perfect match to his dark shaved hair. He wore the same faded jeans, pulled up high around his waist for days at a time.

When I brought home my first report card, my mother handed it off to my father. There was a box checked which indicated that my progress was "not satisfactory." My father attributed my poor progress in school to what he deemed to be my misbehavior, and proceeded to bring correction. I stood in front of him as he announced through screams what he was going to do to me. Then he dramatically whipped his thick, black leather belt out from his jeans and began waving it in the air before whipping me with it. The hits were strong, each lick painfully penetrating through my body. With each blow, it felt like my spirit was melting.

"What do you think about this?" he screamed, his dark eyes glaring down upon me, white bubbling saliva running out of the corner of his mouth from rage. I dared not answer him, except to beg him to stop. I was terrified and urinated in my pants. My mother was enraged when she saw the puddle on the kitchen floor, shoved me away, and scratched me with her long fingernails. My father continued to whip me for misbehaving at school.

"Please believe me!" I begged through the tears, whimpering and sobbing into dry heaves; but my father's punishment was relentless. After the whipping session, my father took his huge hand and slapped me across my small face multiple times to ensure "I got the message." With my ears ringing from the slaps and the pain echoing through my head, my nose bled profusely from all the blows. I felt completely broken and rejected.

Throughout my first year of school, I could garner only average grades. When I moved into the second grade, before each whipping session, my father made me remove my pants and underwear before whipping out his belt. He would reach in his rear pocket, pull out his used red and white bandana handkerchief that smelled like him, and throw it in my face. "You're going to need this!" he would shout. How thoughtful of him. He was never satisfied until I had a bloody nose and puddles of urine on the floor. When my nose stopped bleeding, my mother made me clean up the floor, then she took the blood-soaked bandana and disgustedly threw it in the garbage. While those beating sessions were going on, my mother watched and piped in with words that were as painful as the beatings. She did intervene once, shouting to my father, "That is enough!" My father responded by slapping her in the face with the back of his hand, knocking her eyeglasses several feet away to the floor. She never intervened again.

My parents reiterated how worthless I was to them every chance they got. During my early years, I experienced a combination of frustration, rejection, fear, and neglect, all intertwined in a dark place within me. My desire was for my parents to spend quality time with me and teach me new things, like how to tie my shoes. My father hovering over me and screaming at me while I tried to learn how to tie my shoes left me sitting in a little heap. I desperately tried to see through my tears to tie the laces. I repeatedly tried to wind the laces around my small fingers to make loops. My ears rang from my father's screaming and belittling me with crushing names, eventually knocking me to the ground in disgust. I used to stand in front of a mirror just to see how it felt to be seen. Retreating to the barn was where I found a refuge amongst the sheep and barn kitties. I knew they would do me no harm, and my little soul felt grateful I had a safe place to exist.

One day during school recess, sitting cross-legged beside my friend Sarah, she asked, "What do you want to be when you grow up Deb?"

"Oh, that's easy," I said, as we twirled yellow dandelions between our little fingers while the sun shone warmly down on us. "I'm going to own my very own farm someday and be a professional shepherd!" I replied with conviction. They say, when you know, you know, and that I did! As soon as I could walk, my destination was the sheep barn. I always believed my destiny in life was to serve as one of God's shepherds on this earth; to care for, promote, and enhance his special four-legged creatures called sheep.

Most sheep are highly intelligent creatures, many having distinct personalities and feelings. They identify with their shepherd through their voices and physical actions towards them. They are naturally timid towards humans, but once a trust factor is established, the trust will always exist unless it is broken.

Each spring, there was a "Flattened by Sheep" event where the sheep which had been running free for weeks in the 20-acre pasture were rounded up for shearing time—the annual removal of their wool. Each female sheep (ewe) weighed an average of 150 pounds and a large group of them were rounded up to be herded into the "catch pen." The catch pen was composed of wood or steel panels measuring approximately five feet long and forty inches high. A corner catch pen was designed to drive the sheep into, then once they were in, one panel was swung shut and tied to secure them.

When I was seven years old, weighing a fraction of the weight of those big heavy sheep, my father assigned me the job of holding the catch pen gate shut to not let the sheep escape. I don't know why he didn't just tie the gate shut, but I was in position to fulfill my responsibility.

After a lot of yelling and screaming in multiple attempts to round up the flock, they were finally corralled into the pen. Still spooked from the stress of being caught, the flock pushed against the gate trying to regain their freedom and return to the distant pasture. I watched as my father ram rodded some of the sheep to capture one, which caused chaos amongst the rest. Some tried to jump over the back of another to escape being handled, pushing as hard as they could against each other. Some were knocked off balance, and the whole time that was going on, a lot of pressure was being put on the gate. As my father attempted to grab one ewe, she made her leap for freedom against the gate I was trying to hold upright. They were much more powerful than me and I realized how futile it was for me to attempt to hold them back. Down came the gate, with me underneath, knocking the breath out of me.

I laid on the ground beneath the flattened gate as the rest of the flock stampeded out at full speed. I could feel the pounding of the sharp hooves piercing and pounding my chest, arms and legs with each passing sheep as I lay helplessly beneath the gate. After being traumatically trampled under the frantic flock, I could finally sit myself upright. As soon as I stood up, my father grabbed my braids and flung me back on the ground, screaming at me for my ineptness. I was horrified because I knew I would be blamed and pay a fierce penalty for allowing the flock to escape. Over time, it became difficult for me to distinguish between the bruises I received at home from the ones I received from being hit and kicked on the school bus. The stresses and struggles of my young life were just beginning.

Throughout my grade school years, no one ever stepped up for me. I am sure many must have suspected my home life was far from normal, but it was a different time back then. People did not want to get involved. Everyone knew my father was not a nice man to deal with, which may be why no one ever intervened on my behalf.

My sister and I were the only farm kids in our area that rode the school bus. We always had extensive farm chores to complete before and after school. We would inescapably have odors of farm life on us, making us easy targets for bullies. One day, a girl named Korey decided she wanted to beat me up because I smelled bad. She was a few years older than me and came from a very well-to-do family. She epitomized the word bully and because I was the youngest, I was her easiest target. Korey was first to board the bus each day and was always ready to torment me.

One day, she gave me a thrashing, kicking me hard in my legs and punching me. I never dared to tell my parents; they would not believe me anyway. I never tried to defend myself either, for fear my father would accuse me of causing trouble. I was subjected to Korey's attacks for weeks. One afternoon as I stepped off the bus, Korey grabbed my arm and squeezed it until it hurt. "I'm going to tell on you and get you in trouble," she said. It was her usual threat, but I was just relieved to get off the bus and away from her.

On our farm was a large, oval-shaped pond bordered by a beautiful forest of stately Maine pine trees. It was the same grand pond I used to sail my handmade boats on. In the frigid winter months, the pond would freeze over as smooth as glass, creating the perfect ice-skating rink. I found an old pair of skates in the attic, and even though they didn't fit me well, I taught myself to ice skate and discovered it was one of my greatest joys. I was hooked and spent a lot of time alone teaching myself how to do fancy turns and jumps. One of my schoolmates was very athletic and a talented skater as well. Her parents supported her dream of becoming a professional skater, taking her to professional lessons each week in the next town over at a large indoor ice arena. They graciously offered to take me along, but I was very disappointed that my mother would not allow it.

I remember that chilly winter afternoon, as darkness was about to fall, when I had walked down the hill to the frozen pond to skate. I was thoroughly enjoying myself, as carefree as I could be gliding across the ice when suddenly I heard my father screaming at the top of his lungs for me to get up to the house immediately. All I could see was his huge outline, which looked like an ominous black cloud. I could tell by his deep, mean tone that there was big trouble waiting for me. Fear came upon me, and even though I didn't know what I had done, my body began trembling uncontrollably. I contemplated running into the barn and hiding with the sheep, but I knew he would find me and the outcome would be even worse.

Walking back up the hill seemed to be the longest walk ever. With each step I took, knowing that my father was waiting for me, my body became weaker. When I got to the house, my father was standing in the kitchen as usual with his enormous body overshadowing me. As he had done so many times before, he undid his belt, whipping it out of the loops, and waved it over my head. He wanted to demonstrate his power over me and screamed at me to take off my pants and underwear.

"Korey's mother called and told me you beat her up on the school bus this afternoon," he scowled. My little legs gave out from underneath me and I crumpled to the floor on my knees. It felt as if life had temporarily left my body. You could say that I fainted at the mere thought of one more beating session. My father hunched down low to the floor and got right in front of my face. I was too terrified to defend myself. No matter what I said, he would snarl at me with white saliva running out of the corner of his mouth and call me a liar. He was determined to teach me a lesson and brand me as "bad" by using a bright violet spray which was used on livestock to help heal their wounds. The color is highly visible and almost impossible to remove.

"Stick out your hands!" he yelled.

I held out my trembling little hands and he sprayed my fingernails with the livestock spray.

"Now everyone will know you are bad. What do you think about that? Oh, that's right, you have no brains to think."

My father's words were a destructive force on my inner soul. With every beating session, irrevocable harm was being inflicted on my soul. I believed the words I constantly heard from my father. My mother's voice also became an echo in my mind:

"Your body is nothing but a piece of clay. We're going to mold you."

"Your head is only useful for a hat rack."

"You are useless and unwanted."

"Get out of my sight!"

Retreating to the barn, I hid in that old wooden hay crib with my sheep surrounding me. It was my refuge whenever I was beaten. I chewed my fingernails until they were raw. The pain was excruciating, but I was trying to remove as much of the spray paint as I could before I had to return to school. When my father saw what I had done, he repeated the punishment. As I ran back to my hiding place in the barn, I shouted, "I HATE him! I really HATE him!! I should have been too young to understand what the word meant, but my father had taught me what it meant. Later that afternoon, I ran across the road to my neighbor's house. With my eight-year-old perception of distance, running across the road seemed far enough away so that no one would find me. When I reached our neighbor's house, I was hoping that she would throw her arms around me and keep me, so that I would never have to go back home. It was a dream that did not come true. She walked me back home and passed me over to my father.

The next day, my father assigned another job for my sister and me; clean out the full house septic tank. He stated he didn't need to call anyone to have it pumped out, that we could do it. He sat on his tractor seat and lifted the cover off with the tractor bucket and chain. He began screaming at us to grab two five-gallon buckets and "start bailing." The horrid stench of the dark gray and brown vile waste caused us both to vomit. We filled our buckets with the sloppy grotesque substance with small shovels and our bare hands for the next several hours. Father just sat on his tractor barking, "If you were boys, you would have finished by now! My mother sat in her lawn chair on the porch watching.

CHAPTER 2
Momma Jo and Daddy John

My godsend during those times was my mother's mother, Josephine Taft. I called her Momma Jo. She was small in stature but had a magnificent spirit and zest for life. Momma Jo was born in Glasgow, Scotland, and raised in an orphanage along with her four siblings. Her mother passed away during childbirth, and her father, Robert Taft, a sea captain of a large clipper ship, was out to sea two years at a time. Momma Jo was an incredibly special soul. She spoke with a beautiful Scottish accent and always presented herself elegantly. She was an exquisite cook and once owned and operated a successful bed-and-breakfast inn for over fifty years.

Her husband, my grandfather John, who we affectionately called "Daddy John," was a dear gentleman, very muscular and rounder than he was tall. He ran away from his home country, Lithuania, when he was sixteen years old. He spoke with a thick Lithuanian accent and sported short white hair adorned by a neatly trimmed white mustache. Like Momma Jo, he was also an exquisite cook. Daddy John had a wonderful sense of humor and was an expert gardener.

They lived two miles away, in a beautiful home that was so close to the Atlantic Ocean that you could throw a rock from their front porch into the water. Occasionally, my sister and I were fortunate enough to stay with them for a weekend during the winter months.

My sister and I looked forward to the times when our parents went on their trips and Daddy John came to pick us up in his old red car. He pretended to be our chauffeur, opening the car door for us as we climbed into the back seat. Daddy John always made us feel special. We rode in the back seat together. When we arrived, Momma Jo was always waiting to greet us, throwing her loving arms around us and hugging us tightly. Momma Jo saved my life, just by her existence. The first thing she did after giving us the tightest hug was to run a deep warm bath full of bubbles and put us both in it. She let us take as long as we wanted and never rushed us to finish. When we were done, she dried us off gently, then dressed us in beautiful pajamas that made us feel warm, cozy, and cared for. I never wanted to leave her home or her arms.

When we were with Momma Jo, we took long walks along the ocean-side. She loved to be outside, just like I did. We took many brisk five-mile walks in the wintertime, and those were some of my happiest times. Momma Jo was an elegant, gentle, soft-spoken, and kind lady. After our brisk walks together, she made us hot tomato soup and grilled cheese sandwiches. Of course we had hot black tea, that we gleefully drank out of a saucer. When we were at home, my sister and I could never sit at the same dinner table as our parents. However, when we visited with Momma Jo and Daddy John, I had my own brightly colored small wooden red chair at the kitchen table. I felt so special, sitting in my favorite chair and in my favorite spot—next to Momma Jo. The first time I saw a color television was at my grandparents' home. I will never forget how amazed I was the first time Momma Jo turned it on.

Daddy John's flower gardens and immaculate lawns were his pride and joy. God help a weed if one ever appeared in his vegetable gardens. His exquisitely colorful flower gardens were set close to the edge of the main road where many travelers admired them as they passed by. During the summer months, some local teenagers spending summer vacations in cabins nearby thought it would be entertaining to sneak over at nighttime and pick all his flowers. They also dug holes in portions of his lawn that were meticulously groomed.

Daddy John's house had a walk-in cellar that was eye level with his lawn and flower beds. After a few weeks of his garden and lawn being destroyed, Daddy John took action to catch the culprits. One night, he stood in his cellar behind an open window and waited. Sure enough, that very night, three teenage boys showed up to inflict more carnage. The following morning, Daddy John came up to the house looking quite satisfied as he told me the story of the night before. In his thick Lithuanian accent, he said, "I stood in my cellar with my window open and shot their asses with rock-salt! They grabbed their asses as they ran away crying and screaming!" His big belly jiggled as he told me his story. He brought his flower beds and lawn back to perfection and had no further problems with teenage summer mischief.

Momma Jo never wanted to learn how to drive, so one day she asked Daddy John to drive her and me to town. I was over the moon excited about going with her, and it was a trip to remember. Momma Jo held my hand as we walked into the only shoe store in town. She showed me all the beautiful shoes for little girls, and I was overjoyed. I had never seen anything like one particular pair of shiny black patent leather shoes. To my absolute delight, Momma Jo purchased them for me that day and allowed me to wear them out of the store. While I was walking down the sidewalk, I kept looking down at my new shoes, admiring the way they clicked on the pavement as I walked. I had never had a pair of shoes like that in my life. I will never forget how special I felt that day.

Later, I got to spend the night with Momma Jo. At bedtime, she got on her knees beside my bed, and I did the same thing right next to her. We crossed our hands, and she taught me how to say prayers. I was very thankful to her and God for the time I could spend with her, and I said so in my prayers. After our prayer, she tucked me into my special little bed with a beautiful blue satin bedspread. I felt like a princess. Momma Jo opened the window a few inches so that I could hear the ocean waves slipping in on the rocks. All of my senses came alive as the cool, fresh, salty air blew through the room and the sound of the ocean waves lulled me to sleep.

When it was time to return home after visiting with Momma Jo, I cringed. Momma Jo did not approve of my mother marrying my father and I could feel the distance between her and my mother. Momma Jo witnessed my father's temper early in their relationship and she was fearful about what the future would bring. I know she must have known that the only time we were bathed was when we visited her, but she never spoke of our home life, ever. I only remember one time when Momma Jo briefly came into our house, but she never once stepped foot in my bedroom.

When Daddy John was in his eighties, his eyesight had suffered a significant loss over the years. One day, he sat in his old red car, ready to go for a drive. I heard him shouting, in his thick accent, a barrage of words which I believed were curse words. He was so frustrated and shouted, "Where the hell is the steering wheel?" I looked to see what was going on and there was Daddy John, sitting in the back seat of the car. It became very apparent to everyone that Daddy John should no longer be driving.

CHAPTER 3

Let Them Eat Cake

Our house was old, built in the 1700's and the primary source of heat was a wood stove on the first floor in the kitchen. The ceiling in my bedroom, which was located upstairs, was constructed of old rotting slim wooden slats slathered in plaster. The roof had leaked badly for so many years that chunks of wet plaster covered in mold continuously fell on my bed and the surrounding area. After supper, when it was time to retire to my cold bedroom, my mother demanded that I kiss my father good night. How I loathed that time of day, but if I refused, it resulted in punishment. I kissed my father on the cheek as an act of duty, not nearly one of love, and I often wondered what it would feel like to have a father show love and affection for me.

The blanket on my bed was an old yellow stained sheepskin. Thankfully, my little body fit underneath it perfectly. Tabby, an orange cat that came in from the barn with me, was my best little friend and confidant. She slept on top of my blanket, making me feel as if someone loved me. Many nights, feeling extremely lonely, I struggled to fall asleep. I had a handful of old musty-smelling books with mold on them, but they were my treasures. I appreciated them and used them on many occasions, to help me escape the night. There was a small clock radio next to my bed, but I was forbidden to turn on the radio. I surrendered to the hopeless feeling of loneliness and thought my life would always be the way it was. I have vivid memories of sobbing and repeatedly uttering the words "I want a Mummy," while banging my head on my pillow until I eventually fell asleep out of sheer exhaustion.

As if having a hard time falling asleep wasn't bad enough, I remember times when I finally fell asleep only to have my mother barge into my room carrying a scotch tape dispenser. She would shout, "You will not be pretty if your ears stick out!" She would tear pieces of tape off, push my ears back until they touched flat to my head and attach several pieces of tape to my ears. When she was done taping them back, she disappeared downstairs. That happened a lot. As my hair grew longer, my mother never allowed me to wear it down or loose. "Boys will look at you with your hair down," she threatened; so, I always wore it up or braided.

If I woke up during the night and noticed some of the tape coming unstuck, I taped it back in place for fear that my mother would think I took it off. Mornings were tough and painful as I tried to get the tape out of my hair. I just used a pair of scissors and cut my hair off in bunches, giving the kids at school another reason to pick on me.

I became ill often and was shut in my room for the entire day alone. I was left with a bucket by my bed which only got emptied when I was well enough to do it myself. The scent made me feel even worse. Fixating on the old wooden door to my room, I hoped for someone to come in, but it never happened until my sister came home from school. I was grateful to see her walk in with toast and cola for me.

I was very creative and resourceful in my younger years, and I wanted to learn how to cook after watching Momma Jo's exquisite talents. She was such an inspiration to me, and I wanted so much to be like her. I remember one day after school I thought I could sneak in a small amount of time away from my farm chores to try to bake a cake. I felt it would be a way to garner some attention and approval. I was excited to try out a new skill and surprise everyone. When my mother came into the kitchen, she became angry that I was not doing farm chores that needed to be done. She grabbed the bowl of batter from me and dumped all of it into the garbage can. "Go outside and do your firewood chores and don't you ever do this again!" she demanded. That put a cold damper on any enthusiasm to learn to cook for many years. I simply was not allowed to. I realized, in the eyes of my parents, I existed to work, and that was the extent of my being. Momma Jo never knew about that experience, so perhaps she thought I had no interest in learning to cook. When I was visiting with her, I loved looking at some of her beautiful cook books filled with enticing colorful pictures and dreamed of having skills like hers. I never got to spend enough time with her to learn more.

Things changed little as I entered high school. I continued to get beat up by mean kids because I smelled like the farm I lived on, only to return home to another shade of abuse. I ran multiple scenarios through my mind of how I could run away and where I would go. However, the fear of being hunted down and caught by my father was far more frightening. I was simply too afraid to leave.

CHAPTER 4

My Beloved Porgy

Living on a large sheep farm, there were always baby lambs that had been rejected by their mothers at birth for assorted reasons. Some mothers simply did not like their newborn lambs, or it could have been a case where the mother could not provide enough milk. As a result, some of those baby lambs became orphans, or as they are referred to in the livestock world, "bummers."

On the flip side, I have seen mother sheep deliver a set of triplets and love the newborn lambs so much that she would not only gloat over her lambs, but she would also try to steal other nearby newborn lambs! It was always my responsibility to care for the orphans, and I enthusiastically took on that task. Those fragile little orphan lambs created a bond with whomever stepped into the role that their mother neglected. With those orphan lambs, I was their caretaker, and they immediately bonded with me. They were all beloved to me, and I gave each one a special name and considered each one my friend. I would have from ten to fifteen orphans in my group and I had a special cozy stall just for them to live in. They were very fragile and had to be separated from the other sheep. Sheep instinctively know which lambs are orphans, so I kept them from being bullied or killed. I shook out beautiful thick yellow straw to create bedding for the orphans and I tried to keep them as warm as possible. Baby lambs lose over half of their body fat immediately after being born, so it was imperative that they be kept warm. Since they didn't have the thick wool of their mothers to cuddle up to for body warmth, I hung an overhead heat lamp for them to sleep under. The highest percentage of baby lamb deaths is because of hypothermia and starvation if they do not receive the required heat and milk in their bellies within their first hour of life.

Sheep determine by smell, under their own lamb's tails, which lambs are theirs. Orphan lambs often tried to steal milk from whoever they could, but that always resulted in them being thrown against a wall or trampled, which is why I had to keep watch over them in a separate pen. I hand mixed special powdered lamb milk with warm water and fed them with the same baby bottles used for humans. The first two weeks of their lives, they had to be fed every three or four hours around the clock. It took a great deal of tender care, time, and dedication for the lambs if they were going to survive. My lambs immediately bonded with me, recognized my voice, and reacted positively to my affection—as any soul would.

One cold February day, an exceedingly small lamb was born as a twin and his mummy wanted nothing to do with him. He was a "runt," and was half the size he should have been. The mother sheep pushed him against the wall, trying to hurt him. I removed him from her and placed him comfortably in my orphan pen. I named him Porgy. Porgy weighed in at approximately four pounds, but he had the spirit to survive. As long as he was on my watch, I was going to do my best to make sure nothing happened to him.

Porgy was a Southdown breed, known for meek personalities with looks that could melt any heart. He had chocolate brown legs, a mouse-colored grey face with tiny little wool curls all over him. His eyebrows were thick and bushy with his little ears flopping down, almost covering his soft deep gentle brown eyes. His tiny voice resembled a stuffed toy with a soundbox in it. He could have been placed on a shelf in a toy store and it would have been difficult to differentiate between him and the stuffed toys. He immediately responded to his name and my voice. When he saw me approaching him at feeding time, you could see the anticipation as he hopped to his feet and wiggled and shook his little tail back and forth with glee. Porgy was on the bottle for eighty days, and during those days we became the best of friends. It was as if we shared a lot in common. We adored each other and formed an unbreakable bond. Over my lifetime, it is safe to say I have raised over two hundred orphan lambs, but I never had one I loved more than Porgy. When I think about the poem, "Mary had a little lamb . . . and everywhere that Mary went, the lamb was sure to go," I think about me and Porgy. We ran and played together. When spring arrived, Porgy walked beside me smelling fresh spring flowers and pulling on green grass blades with his baby teeth like he knew what he was doing. When it was time for him to return to his orphan pen at night, he cried like a baby being separated from me. Finally, he would fall asleep under his nice warm heat lamp. As he drifted off into dreamland, his small legs and brown lips trembled, and I imagined he was dreaming about how we ran and played that day.

Each October, Maine residents looked forward to the largest fair of the year, the Fryeburg Fair. On the last Saturday of the fair, the largest livestock parade in the state was held with over 1,000 head of prize-winning livestock lined up to be showcased. There was always such a variety of livestock paraded in front of the grandstand. Many wore their championship ribbons, to the delight of some and the envy of others as everyone watched the parade. There were draft horses, several in six-horse hitches pulling grand wagons with saddle horses adorned in bright colorful costumes for the gala. They were followed by dairy cattle, beef cattle, oxen, goats, and, of course, sheep. The parade included colorful floats, local high school bands, and all the usual parade entries. There was always lots of music, making it the perfect grand parade.

My little Porgy was still too small to achieve show status. He didn't have the high level of genetics required to win a blue ribbon either, but no one could beat his cuteness factor. I entered Porgy and me into the parade under the entry of "Little Bo Peep." I wore the bonnet and dress, and carried a shepherd's cane with a long flowing pink ribbon hanging from it. I had made a little ribbon halter that functioned as a leash to put on Porgy. We resembled the children's book image to a tee. We lined up for the parade behind the massive and beautiful winning specimens. When the parade attendant blew the whistle, Porgy and I proceeded onto the racetrack in front of thousands of spectators. Each parade participant walked around the entire racetrack, giving the huge crowd lined up along the parade area a great view. My dear Porgy walked gleefully beside me as proud and happy as he had done so many times. His short little legs could not cover the ground quickly, so I walked slowly, listening to the crowd that was overjoyed to see us. "How adorable," I heard many of the spectators say, as we took in the constant clapping and whistling from them. We were the quintessential pair, and I could not have been more proud or happier. The parade announcer stopped us in front of the audience and announced that Porgy and I were the winners in the "Most Authentic" category!

The local newspaper photographers surrounded us, and as the weeks went by, our picture was published in many papers. I still have our picture from the parade that day on my wall. Of all the national champion awards I have won over the years, the one I won with Porgy will always be my treasure. To me, Porgy did not need to win a blue ribbon for all to see that he had won a special place in my heart as the best champion there ever was.

The following day we returned home from the fair to a dusting of snow on the ground. I had great plans for Porgy and looked forward to watching him grow over the winter and maturing to his best potential. A few nights later, I was awake in bed, listening to my sister and father engaged in a loud conversation. It was as if they wanted me to hear it. My father told my sister of his plans to process a batch of lambs for the meat customers, when I heard my sister say "I think we need to butcher that Porgy lamb." My heart sank in horror.

"Yes! That's a good idea," my father replied. I lost my breath and felt my heart breaking. I thought, "This can't be true! This can't be happening!" I froze, and it felt like my blood had stopped running through my body.

I knew if I dared to question my father I would be punished; but I had to plead for Porgy's life–he was my friend! I gathered the courage to pull myself out of bed and went down the stairs, my body shaking in fear, to beg my father not to kill Porgy. Tears streamed down my face, my body trembled in fear as my father zipped his heavy leather belt off his pants and waved it in front of me. He scornfully threatened to use it on me if I did not get back upstairs. My pleading and opinion meant nothing. I felt utterly helpless.

The next day, my father readied his workshop to butcher a group of lambs. He hopped on his tractor, with a chain hanging off the bucket on the front, and drove it over to the barn. I was already there, hoping against all odds that if I were there, he would not take my beloved Porgy. I had never felt more afraid in my young life than I did at that moment. It was my last-ditch effort to plead for Porgy's life. I was sobbing so hard I lost my breath. My father flung open Porgy's stall door, reached in and grabbed him by a handful of his wool from behind his tiny neck. He dragged him out to the tractor as Porgy's little legs flailed, trying to regain his balance. Little Porgy had never known anyone's mean hand on him. He could not fight the strength of my father's firm grip as he wrapped the chain dangling from the tractor bucket around Porgy's neck. In an instant, he tightened the chain, pulled a pistol out of his pocket and shot Porgy right in front of me. He got on his tractor, pushed the hydraulic lever, and I watched in absolute horror as my best friend dangled by his neck. I saw the blood running out of his nose, leaving a red trail in the snow as my father drove him to the workshop to butcher him. My sister was standing at the workshop. Just like my father, showing no emotion whatsoever, she waited to help him process the lambs. My body went limp, as though I had been the one shot. I ran into the woods and kept running until I ran out of breath and fell under a tree. That day, I learned first-hand what genuine pain and loss felt like. My childish heart and eyes should never have experienced those images, and they have never left me. I loathed my father and my sister for doing what they did to my precious little best friend, who I had nurtured from birth.

Debby Jo and Porgy

CHAPTER 5

Farm Kids Security

Between the grueling farm chores and the persistent beatings endured from my father, there were also moments of fond memories. Aroostook County in northern Maine, is so large the states of Connecticut and Rhode Island can fit in it. Stretching for miles, with nothing to see or do, the region was renowned for its high potato yield. Every August, it hosted the Presque Isle Fair which provided great entertainment for the area. A high chain link security fence was installed around the entire perimeter of the fairgrounds, and in the opposite corner of the fairgrounds were the sheep barns. The main gate, where admission tickets were sold, was the only access point for vehicles and pedestrians entering the fair, but a few of the local kids snuck in without paying.

There was a dirt path leading to a dark corner behind the sheep barns, and that path was well known to the local kids. It was the perfect spot for them to dig a hole just deep enough to crawl through on their bellies and gain entrance to the fair without purchasing a ticket. That is where our summer fun began.

The local kids would use heavy-duty fence cutters to cut an opening in the chain link security fence. A group of about twelve of us sheep and cattle kids planned a strategy to discourage them from infiltrating the fairgrounds. On the night that the fair opened, our farm kid security team went into action to fortify the local's secret entrance.

During the day, the farmers collected manure (they referred to it as "tickets") from the cow barns and threw it into wheelbarrows. There were a lot of cows in the barn, so they produced a lot of tickets. In the evening, right before darkness fell, our farm kids' security team gathered to prepare for intruders.

Throughout the day farmers always left behind the wheelbarrows of fresh tickets. We pushed two of the wheelbarrows, full of fresh, soupy, and still steaming manure into a wide hole we dug a few inches from the secret entrance. Once the intruders crawled through the entrance on their bellies, they would immediately fall into the hole containing our fresh pile of tickets. Our farm kids' security team created an additional layer of security for those who persevered despite falling into the manure and thinking they were free.

Ten feet away from the manure pit, we set up three trip lines. We tied hay string low to the ground, from the chain-link fence to the sheep barn poles. Next, we covered the lines with hay so they could not be seen. The fence ran parallel to the barn with a twenty-five-foot-wide alley between the two. The alley also ran the length of the barn. It was the only route the intruders could take to disappear into the carnival, creating a perfect fortress for our "wing backs" to get set up.

Water faucets were stationed throughout the length of the barn. Each of us armed ourselves with long water hoses and hid in the barn with nozzles ready to fire once the intruders tripped the line. We waited anxiously for the cover of darkness to fall. Soon, we saw shadows and heard giggling as the intruders made their way to the entrance. There were usually small groups of two or three people at a time sneaking through the secret entrance. It was easy to tell the moment they slithered down in the cow manure because there was always ear-piercing whaling and screeches of horror! Many turned around and scrambled back through the hole as fast as they could, but most were determined to continue. Once they hit the trip lines, the screaming and squealing continued as we let the cold water flow fast and furiously from the hoses! The livestock superintendent, who oversaw the cattle and sheep exhibitors, endorsed our genius plan. Some evenings he sat out of sight in a lawn chair and watched our plan in action; belly-laughing so hard he almost fell out of his chair.

In gratitude for our help in saving the fair money on lost ticket sales, the superintendent gave each of us free ride tickets for the carnival on the last night of the fair. Those were hilarious memories that we looked forward to every year because we knew there would always be a fresh batch of newcomers that were not aware of the farm kids' security team. We knew how to use our resources, and we had fun doing it!

CHAPTER 6

FRANKLY SPEAKING

A wonderful gentleman named Frank Guston holds a special place in my heart as one of my all-time favorite characters. I first met him at a sheep show when I was eight years old. Frank, an 85-year-old thin and frail shepherd weighing a mere 95 pounds with thinning white hair and eyebrows, was the epitome of meek, humble, and kind with a heart of gold. When he smiled, you could see the couple of teeth he still had left in his mouth and his fading blue eyes still exuded mischief. His spirit was that of a youngster, sporting tattered clothes and shoes that had more holes in them than shoelace holes. Frank lived alone on a little farm in Maine and his true love was his sheep and two cocker spaniels, Blackie and Brownie. He had shown sheep all his life, but he never showed them outside of Maine because he could not afford to travel.

Frank rode in an old relic bright yellow wooden panel vehicle, formerly a Coca-Cola delivery truck. He referred to it as his "10-cent truck." It had more miles on it than the odometer could register. He was proud of his twenty-five sheep, even though they were not of high quality, and even he joked about them. "They are so slab-sided they wouldn't make a pot 'o soup!" he would say. When he attended the fairs with his sheep, he made a wooden farm sign out of a crooked piece of plywood, and in bright red letters the sign read "Frank Guston's Sheep." He recounted times when he would go to the bank to get loans for purchasing grain and fuel for his truck, essential for participating in sheep shows. Winning prize money was how he honored his loans and covered his living expenses.

Frank was a contented soul who slept in the cab of his truck each night with both of his dogs curled up beside him. I watched him cook himself a little breakfast each morning in the sheep barn, using an old rusty electric frying pan, and then watched him and his two dogs enjoy their food. The dogs always licked the frying pan dry. Each morning, he walked to the cattle barn with his dented, rusty coffee cup and an old chipped dog bowl to find a dairy cow that was milking. He reached underneath to steal a "tit squeeze of milk," as he called it, into his coffee cup, and then squeeze a little more into the dog bowl. After Brownie and Blackie finished their warm milk, Frank washed out the frying pan with a water hose, and filled it again with water to use for shaving. Dipping his razor into the water, he constantly looked in his truck mirror to ensure he was well-shaven. After that, he rinsed out the frying pan so it would be ready for the next meal.

I often spotted him sleeping by his truck tire on the ground, with both dogs curled up next to him. He eagerly ate any extra food I prepared for him. I loved sitting and listening to his stories about him showing his sheep in his younger days; back when the sheep were transported to the sheep show by train. I relished those times with him and wished I were his daughter. Everyone loved Frank—it was impossible not to. He provided some of the best memories in my life as a young girl.

Some of the sheep exhibitors thought Frank had dementia, but he was sharp as a tack and knew how to take advantage of their thoughts! On show days, he asked me to help him show his sheep because he could no longer hold the stronger ones. I wanted Frank to earn as much money as he could, so I always showed my best for him. I would win a blue ribbon, return the sheep to its pen and wait for Frank to pass me another sheep to show for the remaining classes for that breed. There are a variety of sheep breeds which look similar, but a seasoned breeder can tell the difference by such features as skull structure, length of ears, or general body structure. Half of Frank's sheep had black faces; the other half were white-faced. When it was time to show the black-faced breed, he picked the ones he wanted me to show for him. When it was time to show his white-faced sheep, we followed the same process and did well each time. Frank did not have a qualifying breed when they rotated back to the black-faced category, so he passed me a sheep he knew I had already shown earlier.

"Frank, we already showed that one!" I would tell him.

He would fling his hands around, acting confused, and say, "Deb, just take this one!" Reluctantly, I did as he asked. I showed his one set of black-faced sheep as one breed, then later in the day I showed the same ones again as a different breed. He did the same with the white-faced sheep. Not even the judge noticed. Back then, the fairs were so laid back they did not hire major league judges, so the ones they hired either didn't notice or didn't care about discrepancies. There was no bookkeeping, per se, and the judges were just there for a paycheck. Frank knew how to work the system when everyone thought he was just senile! As he would say, "We just turned them around and ran 'em again!"

Frank passed away two weeks after his last show at ninety. "As long as I'm alive, I'm going to attend sheep shows," he always said. And he did. I have his photo in my special sheep scrapbook and over his picture it reads "My hero, Frank." I will forever cherish those memories.

CHAPTER 7

My Beloved Nell

No sheep farm is complete without a highly trained, efficient working border collie sheepdog. These dogs are highly bred in Scotland and England to help herd sheep. They are born and raised amongst thousands of sheep, and it is their instinct to drive and round up sheep. That is their purpose.

I was thirteen years old when my father ordered a female border collie puppy from one of the nation's most accomplished breeders in the Midwest. Over the years, the breeder had imported select dogs from both Scotland and England and had won two world championships in the sheepdog trials competitions.

Arrangements were made to have the new female puppy (Nell) shipped to our farm in Maine. She bonded with me instantly, and we became inseparable. Nell slept with me on my bed every night and we started our day together. Nell performed as she was bred to perform and showed great interest in learning how to help me herd the sheep. It takes an enormous amount of time and patience to train a good working dog on the ins and outs of sheep herding. They need to understand the commands and how sheep think. A well-trained dog will anticipate the erratic movements sheep make while they are being gathered from their pastures. In an adjacent two-acre pasture that bordered the sheep barn, I designed a training area for Nell to learn her skills. I knew it would take a considerable amount of time, over a year, to bring her to a more advanced level, but I was enthusiastic about taking on the project. It was a goal I set for both of us, and we worked very well together.

I set up obstacle courses around the field to teach Nell how to drive the sheep around the gates slowly and over a little bridge I made. I let three sheep out at a time and taught Nell the commands she needed to learn. "Come-by," was the command to move clockwise around the sheep. "Away to me," was the command to move counterclockwise, and "Come in steady," means to drive the sheep forward to me slowly. "That'll do," means our work is done. In our two-hour sessions every single day for months, Nell and I made significant progress. After training, we played together. Nell was golden in every sense of the word — personality, beauty, and superior intelligence.

After training Nell for about a year, I had her working the sheep beautifully! In one of our practice sessions, I knew she had matured into a stunning working dog and had been trained well enough to compete at an elevated level. I had increased the number of sheep we trained with from three to five. Sheep always group with odd numbers, and if there are even numbered sheep loose in a pasture, one will always break off and separate from the group. That is why in professional dog trials, you only see groups of three or five sheep being used.

One day while Nell and I were in the field training, Bob, who occasionally stopped by to visit the sheep and see the goings on at the farm, paid us a visit. My father, who was walking towards the house, stopped to have a conversation with him. Bob noticed Nell and I doing our practice session across the pasture, and he was thoroughly entranced. He walked over to the fence and silently observed as we performed our training routine.

Nell did a remarkable job herding her group in circles, through open gates, over the bridge, one sheep at a time, and driving them away from me. Then, "making the fetch," she drove them back to me. I made a large circle with white lime powder and trained Nell to bring the sheep into the circle and keep them still, for at least one minute. They had to remain still until I could touch one without it walking out of the circle. Every single one of those movements was mandatory in competitions. For thirty minutes, Bob watched as Nell performed an arduous task of keeping the sheep still while staring them down. We delivered an award-worthy performance, then I gave Nell the "That'll do" command which meant it was quitting time. With a big smile on her face and her thick black fluffy white-tipped tail wagging, she leaned her body against mine. She was so proud of herself, and I was proud of her too. I was beaming with pride at our performance.

Bob was incredibly impressed and complimented us on our well-orchestrated demonstration. "Deb, you have done a remarkable job," he said, as Nell and I exited the pasture. "I trained that dog," my father snapped. "I taught her everything she knows."

When I heard those words, it took my breath away. My father had taken credit for what I had worked so diligently to achieve. He robbed me of a glorious moment, and I was devastated. I remember walking back to the barn with a feeling that my heart had fallen deep into my stomach. When I got to the barn, I sat on a bale of hay and sobbed.

My Beloved Nell

CHAPTER 8

Hells Angels

I was doing a safety check of the pasture at the far end of the farm where sixty sheep were grazing. The pasture was about a quarter of a mile away and when I got there, I came upon a terrible scene. Stray dogs had gotten into the pasture and attacked and killed six of the ewes that were pregnant with lambs. Word had gotten around the neighborhood that the dogs were owned by a group of Hells Angels that lived about three miles away. They were known as notorious 1% bikers with a criminal element. A few days later, the dogs returned and chased the sheep again. My father was near the pasture when the dogs returned and shot them dead. Their collar tags identified their owners. A few days later, we heard a loud rumbling sound that got closer and closer, rattling the walls in the kitchen. My father looked out the window and saw several Harley-Davidson motorcycles turning into our driveway. The news had traveled that their dogs had been shot when they did not return home. My father told my mother to hide in her bedroom; he threw on his jacket and said to me, "You answer the door," as he slipped out the back door to hide.

The knocks on the door were not gentle knocks. They sounded hard-driving as they pounded with clenched fists. I was shaking from pure fear when I opened the door. There stood at least ten bikers in front of me wearing their black leather vests, some adorned with thick chains with "Hells Angels" in large letters across the back. They had long hair and beards, wore dark-shaded glasses, and did not appear friendly. "We heard our dogs got shot!" one of them shouted at me. I do not remember what my answer was, but I remember the fear of God running through me while I made an excuse, explaining why my father was not at home. My father did not have the courage to face the men himself. The interrogation was sharp and real, and I thought my legs would give out from underneath me.

Soon after that visit, several things happened around the farm to my father's equipment. Fuel was stolen, water added in gas tanks, fuel lines cut, and several things came up missing.

"A Hells Angel never forgets what they consider an injustice."

CHAPTER 9

Sawmill Trauma

Our farm was two miles away from the Atlantic Ocean and bordered a fishing village. There was a tremendous demand for lobster traps, so my father opened a sawmill to manufacture them. In the state of Maine, the only wood that could be used for lobster traps was oak. Oak is an extremely heavy wood, but because of its strength to withstand the heavy forces and moisture of the ocean waters, it was the most suitable and durable wood. My father hired twenty men to work at the sawmill to process the large oak logs into smaller pieces. Maine was rich with a bountiful abundance of oak, and several truckloads of logs were ordered each week for delivery. The six-foot logs, weighing several hundred pounds each, were off-loaded and piled onto a 50-foot-long elevated land dock called a "brow." The log trucks used hydraulic grapplers, which were installed on their big trucks, to grab and lift each log, then set the logs down on the brow platform to be rolled into the main saw.

To make the logs more workable, the first stage of processing was using the main saw to saw them down. Two full-time men were assigned the task of manning the 42" circular saw. Part of their job was to roll the logs approximately 32 feet from the brow to the main saw. The lobster traps were assembled on the second floor of the mill, then once completed they were slid down a ramp, out a side door, and onto delivery trucks. Hundreds of lobster traps were delivered locally or a little further out to Martha's Vineyard, another booming lobster industry area near Cape Cod, Massachusetts.

At thirteen, my father had me relieving two of the sawmill workers when I got home from school. It saved him money because he did not have to pay another man to do the task. While most kids my age got to play sports or games after school, I was expected to do an extremely dangerous job. One worker, Bill, whom I was assigned to relieve, was a retired lobsterman. He taught me how to use a wood hook to hook and roll the logs properly. I climbed up onto the brow and looked up at a stack of logs five times taller than me. Just one of those logs outweighed me by several hundred pounds. I quickly learned how to hook the logs, then accurately and efficiently drop them down. Each log landed with a loud crash as it tumbled down on the platform and rolled up to the main saw.

Once I had filled the long brow up to the main saw, my father gave me another task of working on a strip saw. A middle-aged man, Cecil, was an incredibly industrious worker and also a lobsterman, who operated the strip saw. He worked like a bear and had a high expectation that whoever was on the receiving end of the saw would do the same to keep up with him. The slabs of oak that reached the strip saw phase of processing often weighed over forty pounds each. In the winter, when they were covered with ice and snow, they were especially hard to manage, even after the wood had run through the saws. Cecil pushed the slabs one at a time, hard and fast, back-to-back, non-stop. Through the enormous shrilling sharp blade of the strip saw, clouds of sawdust blew into the air and, chunks of wood would fly out from the blade. My responsibility was to pull each heavy slab out of the saw and slide it back across the table to Cecil as fast as possible so he could keep stripping it down to size. I did that job for hours.

One afternoon, after a few hours of grueling work, I heard a loud grinding noise. A frozen chunk of wood got caught in the saw blade, and a splintered piece of the wood whirled out towards me and pierced my forehead, lacerating my scalp. When Cecil saw blood running profusely down my face, he shut the saw down. I ran back to the house, holding back tears, frightened and in pain. I was hoping my mother might be there to help me, but no one was home. I laid down on my bed, trying to stay quiet as I packed several cold wet towels on my head to try and stop the bleeding myself. My mother returned home a few hours later and deemed that, despite my need for stitches, no doctor visit was necessary. Since I was denied proper care, it took quite a while for my head wound to heal. I still carry that scar on my forehead as a reminder of the sawmill days. Not long after that incident, the same thing happened to my father. He made his way back over to the house and my mother took him to the hospital immediately where he was seen and given stitches. Juggling farm chores and millwork exposed me to the demanding nature of work. I shouldered the weight of responsibility, resulting in many challenging days. I always tried to stay cheerful, but inside I was longing to just be able to do kid things. My life seemed destined to work for my father. Whenever visitors came, I was instructed to smile and act happy—or else. Before my father left for one of his getaway trips with my mother, he normally assigned me the duty of performing safety checks in the entire mill.

During the last thirty minutes of each day, the men were required to shut down the machines and clean around each saw. Each night, it was my job to check that all the blowers on multiple saws had cooled down and had no sawdust sitting on top of them. It was also my job to ensure that each saw was unplugged, and all air compressors were off and cooled. I was so afraid if I missed something and a fire started during the night, I would be responsible. My life would surely have been over had that occurred.

At the end of each day, there were chunks of non-usable wood that had been discarded into a large pile across the road from the mill. I saw an opportunity to start a little firewood business with those scraps. I made a wooden cradle on legs, laid down two long pieces of hay string on the bottom, and stacked pieces of wood from the huge pile into my cradle. I tied strings tightly around each bundle and stacked them alongside the road with a handmade sign: "Firewood for Sale—3 bundles for a dollar." It was an honor system, so I left a glass jar on a table for people to leave money for the wood. We lived near a popular tourist town on the ocean, where summer camps were always filled with visitors. The campers always needed firewood, so it was a perfect little business. Business was so good I hired two other kids to help me. It was exhilarating and made my long days in the mill more bearable.

CHAPTER 10
Out of Sight, Out of Mind

For a long time, I had been yearning for an opportunity to buy a horse. A friend of mine had a beautiful brown horse for sale and I was saving the money I earned from selling firewood to buy him. Batch was gentle and sweet with a beautiful snow-white blaze that ran down the front of his face. The farm that owned him called to have him delivered to our farm, but when I counted my money, I was $75 short. My parents showed no interest and did not offer to help me with the additional money I needed. I worked long hours into the night by flashlight, bundling as much wood as I could to make up the extra money. It took a few more months, but I finally had enough money to buy Batch. I purchased a new leather bridle, an old used saddle, and some grain to feed him. I was thrilled and proud that I did it all on my own. The day the big truck off-loaded him and passed him to me was the greatest joy in my life.

Batch provided an enormous source of happiness and freedom for me. He gave me a reason to get all my chores done quickly so I could steal away and go for long, beautiful rides with him. I rode him to the ocean and through trails in the forest. I had the freedom of being one with nature, absorbing its sounds and smells, and inhaling the fresh ocean air. These trips through the woods provided me with a sense of being. We ventured down to the end of a dirt road, two miles from where I lived, where two brothers, Noel and Ernest, lived. They were two elderly gentlemen who had both retired from the fast-paced city life to an old house deep in the woods. They preferred to live as far away from civilization as possible. Whenever possible, Batch and I rode to their house to visit. During the winter days, when my parents were away, I made homemade bread, loaded up my leather saddlebag, and took it to my friends in the woods. I loved riding down that dirt road and smelling the fresh bread aroma as Batch and I made our way along the trail. Noel and Ernest anxiously awaited our visits, and as soon as we approached their driveway, they met us outside.

One day, as I was pulling a warm loaf out of my bag, it fell on the ground and spooked Batch. He stepped sideways and landed his hoof right on top of that loaf of bread. It was crushed as flat as a pancake, leaving a distinct horseshoe imprint right on top! I was mortified and felt so bad! One of the brothers laughed out loud, cheerfully picked it up, and said, "It's still gonna taste good!" He gleefully carried the smashed masterpiece into their kitchen while I dismounted and tightened up my saddle. As I mounted back up and turned Batch around to leave, I looked over my shoulder at the brothers. They were both sitting at the kitchen table unwrapping their treat, spreading butter on it. With big smiles on their faces, they were ready to devour it. What a great feeling it was to give them something they loved. That simple act gave me a sense of purpose. They loved my gifts of bread and enjoyed watching Batch and I ride off. Whenever I left, Batch and I put on a little show for them, galloping away at full speed while they clapped their hands in pure joy. Batch and I enjoyed countless trips exploring the woods and looking for new trails. Those were glorious times of exploration spent with just me, nature, and my beloved horse.

During our back road travels, I discovered a very narrow old trail that led directly down to the ocean. The trail was overgrown with trees and thick brush, making it very difficult to navigate. The overhead branches drooped so low that I had to duck down low to get through, otherwise I would scrape my head. I dismounted from my saddle and broke off branches here and there so Batch and I could navigate our way through. One day, I noticed the trail had been newly groomed and cleared of the low-hanging tree limbs. Even the large rocks that had previously blocked the trail had been moved. My friends Noel and Ernest had taken chainsaws and cut big tree limbs back for us. They removed the large rocks, and turned the trail that was once difficult to navigate into a wonderfully smooth pathway for me and Batch. I was overwhelmed with gratitude and thanked them for caring enough to do that. It must have taken them days to complete, and I know it was their way of giving back.

When I wasn't enjoying adventures with Batch, I had to attend to my major chores around the farm. When I got home from school each day, I had to perform all the duties on the list that was waiting for me on the table. One of my first tasks was to take the empty bottles of alcohol that my mother had consumed out of her bedroom closet. I placed them in large black plastic garbage bags, and carried the heavy bags outside. We had a neighbor who frequently watched the goings on from across the road where she lived. I had to take the bags out through the back door because my mother did not want our neighbor to see me emptying the bags of alcohol bottles. Once my chores were completed, my mother would say to me, "Get out of my sight!" Little did I know her plan was to literally and physically get me out of her sight!

"Take this medicine and get to your room!" she snarled. I took the medicine, went to my room, and instantly fell into a deep sleep and experienced a horrific nightmare that I could not wake up from. Every time I obeyed my mother and took the medicine, I experienced the same feeling. I always slept on my side, but when I took the medicine, I remember laying on my back, unable to roll over or even move. My senses went black, and I had a feeling of absolute helplessness. I could not physically move my limbs, and was extremely dizzy. In each instance, I felt like I was in a deep, dark, narrow tunnel that got larger and larger, then smaller and smaller. It tightened around me and almost smothered me. I could not escape from the horrible nightmare that repeated itself. I was not sleeping—I was unconscious. I had a terrible headache, and felt like I was on a high-speed rollercoaster, and as hard as I tried, I could not jump off. Those dark, eerie feelings stuck with me for most of the following day.

It was a frightening, helpless feeling that I never understood until I was older. My mother truly wanted me "out of her sight," so she had drugged me. Although I broke free from those horrible times, I still experience terrible nightmares that always stem back to my childhood.

My protector during those times was my beautiful Siamese cat, Cleo. She was the epitome of beauty with her mahogany brown points and azure blue eyes surrounded by the most affectionate dear heart I ever knew. She was my godsend during those horrible times, and I adored her beyond words. Each night I kissed her sweet face goodnight as she slipped away to sleep on my chest. I crossed my hands over her while saying a special prayer asking God to always take care of her and never let her leave me. She was seventeen years old but as healthy as could be with no issues at all.

We received a phone call with an invitation to show our sheep at a new show that was being held quite a distance away. We would be gone for two weeks, so I prepared a self-feeding dish of dry kibbles for Cleo. I filled a large water bowl and a box with fresh litter, so she would be comfortable until my return. Once the sheep were loaded and we were ready to drive out, my father said he had to do a quick errand. As I waited outside near the truck, I watched him return to the house. After a few minutes, I heard a piercing loud gunshot coming from the back of the house. I did not know what had just happened and was frightened. He appeared from the back of the house and showing no emotion approached the truck. Sliding into his seat he said, "I just took care of Cleo. Get in the truck."

I could not speak. My heart had just been ripped out of me. I sobbed until I lost my breath. My father put the truck in drive and then said, "When your mother and I first got married, for entertainment we would tie our cats' tails together and hang them up on the rafters and watch them try to get away". He was the epitome of cruel and found it amusing. I sensed his evil nature as he laughed while sharing that story with me.

Debby Jo and Batch

CHAPTER 11

No Butterfly Kisses

One of my teachers sent a note home with me stating that she felt I needed to be seen by a doctor. I was pretty ill and my symptoms were so bad that my mother took me in to be seen. She was very irritated, and it was obvious that she did not want to make the ten-mile trip into town. It was the first time I ever remembered seeing a doctor. I prayed I could see him alone in the exam room to tell him what was going on at home, but my mother stayed by my side She knew that if she was with me, I would not dare speak a word about our home life or anything else I had been experiencing. She was correct.

On the drive home, she was extremely angry. The doctor had diagnosed me with mono and a severe case of tonsillitis which needed to be treated with antibiotics and rest. We pulled into the driveway, walked into the house, and she slapped me across my face as hard as she could. "You have the kissing disease, and you should be ashamed of yourself!" she screamed. "Who have you been kissing at school?" I had never kissed anyone, but she was relentless in making me feel like I had done something bad. I was feeling so bad and so weak; I threw my arms around her and begged her to believe me. In my heart, I was longing for her to embrace me and assure me I would feel better soon. Instead, she pushed me away from her chest and said, "You are a tramp and I'm going to send you away." I believed her.

My punishment for being ill was a longer list of chores. That night after seeing the doctor, my tonsils were so swollen they were touching, making it almost impossible to sleep. When I dozed off, I was awakened by my snoring noises. Usually, my mother never checked on me at night, but that night, she came into my room. "I see you're still breathing," she grumbled, then turned away and retreated downstairs. My spirit was crushed, and I spent another night banging my head on my pillow, crying for a mother who cared. For years my mother threatened to send me away, and I always believed she would.

The thought of being sent away terrified me. I remembered a girl who lived with us for a while. All I can remember about her is that she was a few years older than me and had long, dark hair. She stayed in a room upstairs, near my room, and she was in there alone a lot. The only other memories I have of her were the times I heard her crying as my father screamed at her. One day, after returning home from school, she was gone. I never learned what happened to her and was forbidden to speak of her again, ever.

One night, after coming in from doing my chores, I was cold, aching, and still feeling weak. It was on very rare occasions that I could ever take a bath, but I ran warm water in the bathtub to warm up. I have a memory of my mother bending over the tub with me once, briefly, when I was younger. With a washcloth, she firmly told me how to wash. She made it seem more like a punishment than a life lesson on how to care for myself. As I prepared to get in the tub, my mother flung open the bathroom door so hard it dented the wall. "Who are you kissing at school and why do you need to take a bath?" she screamed. "You must be messing around with boys at school. It's the only reason you think you need a bath." I was horrified and fearful, but could not convince her otherwise.

My world plunged into an even darker abyss of hopelessness, and I was never taken to a doctor again. The feelings of rejection, emptiness, angst, and deep fear I experienced as a child never faded from my memory. I will never understand my mother's inability to be a caring mother to me, and that will never be forgotten.

"There's no way to be a perfect mother and a million ways to be a good one."

Jill Churchill

CHAPTER 12
Transition into Adulthood

My sister and I experienced the greatest sense of freedom when my parents went away on their weekend trips, leaving us home alone. We survived by eating frozen TV dinners, feeling like royalty indulging on a delicacy. When it was time for them to return, I always came down with a severe case of diarrhea. Just the thought of going back to the dark times of their presence made me physically ill.

I remember the afternoon I came into the house after being out in the cold doing chores. I was fourteen, but I knew nothing about the changes that occurred in our bodies when we reached a certain age. When I went to the bathroom and saw blood, I was horrified! I did not know about what was happening to me. I was wrought with fear and sought my mother for help. She was disgusted and infuriated with me! The last thing I expected was for her to react the way she did. She displayed neither calmness nor support as she angrily flung open the bathroom bureau drawer. She retrieved a rubber belt contraption, and hurled a woman-sized maxi pad at me. In one quick motion, she snatched the pad and wound it into the rubber belt contraption. Mother yanked it up my leg roughly and scratched my legs with her long dirty fingernails in the process. "Wear it!" she yelled. She slammed the bureau drawer shut and stormed out of the bathroom, slamming the door behind her in disgust. I just stood there frozen, horrified, and confused, feeling like I had done something wrong. My mother said nothing else about my change of life. I found whatever supplies I could in the old wooden bureau drawers in the bathroom. If any woman-sized pads were left in the drawer, I used what was there until they were all gone. My bed sheets were rarely washed, and I was not allowed to wash them myself. The sheets on which I laid had been soaked with blood, then dried. I was aware of my offensive body odor and attempted to discover a fix. I found a bottle of perfume and sprayed my private parts. It burned so badly I was in tears. In my despair and desperation, I snuck over to my neighbor Donna's house to seek advice. She gently explained what I needed to know and pulled a book from her bookcase. "Our Bodies-Ourselves" was a book written by a doctor, targeting teenage girls and covering various aspects of the female body and its functions. "Take this book home and read it from cover to cover," she encouraged. She assured me that if I read that book, it would ease my fears and teach me what I needed to know. I thanked her, slipped the book under my coat, and returned home, going straight to my room. I read the first chapter, absorbing all the knowledge I could, and before I went to sleep, hid the book beside my bed for safekeeping.

The next night, I slipped into my bed to continue reading the book that was teaching me so much about my body. I turned to pull the book out and it was gone! It wasn't long before my mother stepped into my room and scolded me harshly for reading a book like that. "You don't need to read anything like that!" she yelled. Mother demanded that I return the book and never accept anything like that again.

CHAPTER 13
Goodbye Momma Jo

Momma Jo became ill and was admitted to our local hospital; the same one I was born in. Not long after her admission, her doctor informed her that she had end-stage stomach cancer that had progressed rapidly. She knew any kind of treatment would be futile, so she declined treatment. Being the strong independent woman she was, Momma Jo checked herself out of the hospital to return home, where she was happiest. Seeing her lying in her bed so pale and weak broke my heart. Every day, Batch and I rode the two-mile distance to her house just to be with her. Two weeks after she checked herself out of the hospital, she became too weak to even speak. That Thursday, she was readmitted, and her doctor did not think she would survive the weekend. My parents were planning to leave that day to attend a sheep sale in Massachusetts and were not expected to return for several days. My heart was breaking at the thought of my favorite person slipping away. I felt such a disdain for my parents who would dare leave at such a critical time. How could they leave her? I was sure my mother would cancel that trip and stay by Momma Jo's side, but they left me at home alone with Daddy John to comfort him.

Momma Jo and Daddy John met when they were teenagers and had been married for over 65 years. They were inseparable. Daddy John was beside himself, feeling hopeless as he witnessed his beloved mate slipping away. That evening, I drove Daddy John in his old red car to the hospital so we could both be with Momma Jo. We held her hand, one of us on each side of her, and I instinctively knew it would be our last visit with Momma Jo. Daddy John whispered some special things to her in her ear and tenderly said goodbye. He leaned down to kiss her on her beautiful face and quietly slipped out of the room, leaving me alone with her. I told her how much I loved her and thanked her for always being my godsend. I squeezed her soft pale hand to let her know I was beside her, still hurting that her own daughter was not there by her side. Despite her inability to speak, I could sense her awareness of my presence. I quietly tore myself away from her, leaving a substantial portion of my heart with her. Daddy John asked me to take him home, so I had to be strong for him and do what he needed.

I quietly drove Daddy John home, where we sat beside each other on a large rock at his favorite spot overlooking the ocean. We watched the endless waves flow in softly against the rocks that lined his front lawn until the sun quietly fell. I thought my mother would contact us to check in, but she never did. I stayed with Daddy John, who was in his eighties, until darkness came and returned home to do all of the livestock chores. It was almost 11:00 p.m. when Momma Jo's doctor called. He did not ask for my mother, he asked for me. All I remember him saying was that he was so sorry to inform me that Momma Jo had just passed away. He told me she softly called out my name three times and then started to quietly sing, minutes before she passed. Singing was one of her favorite things to do when she was happy. The doctor thought it was remarkable that she called my name and was singing because prior to that moment, she had not been able to speak for days. My grief was inconsolable, and I felt completely helpless. A severe thunderstorm came up, with lightning bolts cutting the dark sky above in every direction as if it were angry. The wind was blowing the doors open and shut, and it was an unnerving feeling as I dealt with a flood of emotions.

I called a friend of Daddy John's who lived in New York City. He kept me calm and helped me figure out a way to track down my parents. I was able to find a telephone number for the sales manager of the event they were attending and explained the nature of my call. He would not be able to get a message to them until the next morning because no one knew where they were staying. Later that day, my mother finally called to tell me they would be home the following day. She insisted that I not give Daddy John the news until she got there, so I had to make an excuse for why I could not take him to the hospital. He knew in his heart—he and I had just lost the love of our lives.

When my mother finally returned home, she demanded that I stay behind at the house while she went to Daddy John to tell him the news. I always wondered what excuse she used to explain her absence. I believe she wanted me to stay behind so I would not be a witness to whatever pathetic excuse she used.

CHAPTER 14

Invitation to Toronto

During my early teenage years, my sheep showing and fitting abilities continued to develop. My passion for sheep and the accompanying activities intensified, with countless competitions adding to my experience. At sixteen, I received a letter from one of the most respected sheep breeders in Canada, the Gartshore family. They had watched me show my sheep in Toronto the year before. I opened the handwritten letter and read an invitation by Mrs. Gartshore, asking if I was available to help them prepare and show their Dorset sheep at the upcoming Canadian National competition, the Royal Winter Fair. They were impressed with my skills with sheep and would love to have me help them compete. They offered to purchase my plane ticket to Toronto, cover all expenses, and pay for my time. It was a dream come true! I telephoned Mrs. Gartshore and accepted their offer. You can imagine the pure elation and excitement I felt to be invited to such a grand show and work with some of the best sheep in Canada, and with a highly respected family. I had never flown on an airplane before, so I had many new experiences ahead of me that lifted my heart enormously. I had a sense of purpose! My parents showed no emotion of my glorious offer and seemed happy that I would be away for a while.

The Toronto Exposition Center, was an immense set of indoor arenas where several thousands of livestock competed. The best of the best traveled from all over to earn major titles and bragging rights for their farms. The competition provided an opportunity for breeders to promote genetic excellence from their breeding programs and stimulate the sale of their livestock. Spectators and agricultural representatives from all over the world traveled to the event to compare their programs, livestock husbandry, and breeding genetics. Multiple agricultural seminars would be held for the attendees throughout the weeklong extravagant event.

The day finally came for me to pack my small suitcase for an adventure and honor of a lifetime. I packed my seven-inch sheep shears in my bag. The flat shears are made of stainless steel with extremely sharp blades. They look like grass cutters but are handmade in England specifically to cut wool. The handles were wrapped in leather for comfort to the hands. This was a necessity not a luxury because we spent hours trimming by hand. I was used to my special hand blades and the way they cut the wool. Just as a barber's tools have value to the barber, my sheep shears were a crucial tool.

I boarded a large plane in Portland, Maine with such anticipation and excitement, and flew directly to Toronto. My eyes had never seen anything like it before. It was my first time traveling to another country. Seeing a large city with such tall buildings was the highlight of my life. The Gartshore family warmly welcomed me, and we proceeded to their designated pens in the sheep arena. I got to work immediately and began fitting their sheep and using the skills that I had learned.

I had the chance to implement my sheep grooming skills and showcase a special process I used which was unknown to many spectators. The sheep must be thoroughly washed a week ahead of the show with warm water and special livestock soap. Their wool must be extremely clean and snow-white to give the appearance of beauty. Their fleeces hold a high percentage of moisture, so it takes a full two days to dry sheep's wool. The next step in the process is to lift them onto a "blocking stand" which is like a dog grooming table. The sheep blocking stands are made of heavy gauge steel and have a hand crank on the front to raise or lower the table to the desired height. The head of the sheep is comfortably rested in a headpiece with a small light strap behind their neck to keep them in place and prevent them from jumping off the stand.

A thorough process of grooming starts with brushing the fleece out and down with a tool called a curry comb to brush out any foreign pieces of hay that might have stuck in their wool. It also starts the wool in a common direction to straighten the fibers out from a natural curl. Another handpiece is used to fluff the wool, called a card with a small paddle-like tool that has small outward curved teeth on it much like a dog slicker brush. This is used to lift and straighten the wool fibers to ready them for trimming and smoothing. Once carded so the wool fibers appear uniform, hand blades are used to trim and sculpt the wool to appear as smooth as possible. One must know the attributes of the individual sheep you are grooming to best highlight their positive points. The process takes about three hours per session and three sessions per show. It is a highly detailed skill that takes years of practice and thorough knowledge to learn how to highlight the best features of the livestock you are preparing for competition. Many individuals have made a professional career of being "fitters." The top performers make a fine living performing their skills with show livestock. Although it requires hard work, diligence, and long hours, the satisfaction of winning top awards and gaining a highly valued reputation makes it worthwhile.

Mrs. Gartshore had six extremely high-quality sheep entered in the competition and I had ample time to spend enhancing their qualities. I hand carved the wool out on each sheep to accentuate all the good points in their body structure, along with making their fleeces look like velvet to catch the judges's eye. I had enough time for the sheep to become familiar with my voice, which is a key factor for sheep handlers. Once we are in the show ring, it is imperative that the sheep trust their handler. Sheep are intelligent creatures, and they associate people's voices with positive or negative behavior. Some sheep love being groomed and shown, and willingly hop right onto the blocking stand, close their eyes, and sleep while being groomed. For some sheep, it is a relaxing process, and they enjoy the attention.

Once the trimming process is complete after each session, they are covered with "show blankets." These coats are made of a lightweight canvas with leg straps sewn into them to keep them from slipping off. They keep the sheep clean until show day. Spectators, who were not familiar with why they are wearing them, made comments such as "Oh look, they are wearing pajamas!" Show day arrived, the arena was bustling with other exhibitors, and thousands of spectators. Visitors walked through the area admiring all the exquisite specimens of livestock that were on display in their stalls before taking their seats in the show arena. The breed of sheep we were showing were Dorsets, the same breed I had grown up with, so my confidence in working with them was solid. I was satisfied with how they looked after my final preparations.

Getting the sheep ready for the first class, I took my hand card, gently patting the wool again to make sure it all looked uniform and level, and brushed any hay off their bellies. I wiped their noses with a wet washcloth and sprinkled a little white baby powder over their ears and knees to cover up any blemishes. The entire process is much like women going to their beautician for a hair appointment. They walk in looking one way but walk out looking fabulous!

Walking into the show arena, I was surrounded by the most glorious sight of pomp and circumstance I had ever seen. The arena, circular in design, seated thousands of people. Many bright red and white Canadian flags hung all around the ring overhead. A live organist was playing music, and the official judge looked dapper in his suit and tie. He wore a Canadian red ribbon badge that said "Official Judge." Witnessing the entire scene was awe-inspiring, evoking a profound sense of pride as a competitor in such a magnificent showcase. I was surrounded by seasoned competitors showing their sheep off to the best of their abilities, all vying for that first-place win. We lined up our entries side by side in the middle of the ring, with the judge standing back about twenty feet, analyzing each one while comparing them to each other. He stepped up to the line to examine each sheep individually from head to toe, opening their mouths to verify their age by their teeth. Next, he ran his hand down the top of their backs to determine their length and straightness while taking into consideration their tail set, which must be extremely high. The judge felt the rear leg muscles of the sheep to determine how thickly muscled they were compared to the next sheep in line. The thicker the muscle, the more desirable they are. Another thing the judge considered was the sheep's growth for their age, along with how well they represent their breed standard. He examined their feet and legs to determine how sound and strong they were in their pasterns (ankles). The judge directed the sheep to walk in a wide circle to view them on the move. He looked for strong rear legs and nice long strides when walking, an important feature to look for in all livestock. All those attributes were critical qualities which would be passed on in genetically progressive breeding programs.

When decision time was close, the judge stood back to get one last look, taking mental notes on the individuals he liked, while deciding how he was going to make his final placings. We were vying for a red ribbon, which, in Canada, was the first-place ribbon. The judge pointed his finger at the individual he wanted to pull out of line to stand on a side profile as his winner. He looked straight at me and gave me that finger point! The rest of the class was then picked one at a time to stand in line behind me. I showed my sheep, holding her head up high and alert, while ensuring all four legs were straight and square underneath her. The show ring steward, wearing a fancy black top hat, passed me the glorious red ribbon for the win in our first class. Over the next three hours, we repeated the same process and won every class in which we were entered. For the grand finale, all first-place winners were paraded back into the middle of the ring while the judge studied and compared them again. The judge strolled over to the microphone and spoke about each individual in front of him, detailing what he admired most about each entry. He complimented the competitors for bringing their sheep up to championship level and was ready to announce the winner. He put the microphone back into its stand and walked a few circles around the group standing before him, giving full suspense to the audience. My focus was split between him and my sheep, as I tried to keep my sheep looking her best. As the judge approached me, he took his hat off and extended his hand to shake mine as the champion!

A fancy red and white satin rosette sash with sparkling large gold letters was laid over the back of my sheep by the ring steward. It read: "The Royal Agricultural Winter Fair – Toronto – Canada – National Champion Ewe." The audience applauded loudly, cheering and whistling. Glancing over to the sideline where Mrs. Gartshore and her family were watching, I saw Mrs. Gartshore wipe tears from her eyes. It was truly the thrill of a lifetime!

The Gartshore family was so elated but humble, as many exhibitors came over to their stalls to congratulate them on such a successful day. They were incredibly grateful and kind to provide me with the opportunity of a lifetime. Because of them I was able to experience such a wonderful moment at an early age. Their sheep were genetically and structurally superior in every way. I was just fortunate to put the finishing touches on them at the end and help them walk away with the grand prize. Suddenly, we noticed a large swarm of people quickly approaching our stalls.

We saw several flashing cameras being held up high and heard screeching as the beehive of people got closer to us. In the middle of the crowd was Prince Phillip from England! Mrs. Gartshore told me he had a sincere love and appreciation for great livestock, so he attended the competition many times over the years. She was not surprised to see him, but she was elated that he was standing at our stalls looking at her winners of the day. Appearing quite dapper, he smiled at us, shook Mrs. Gartshore's hand, and said in a soft English accent "Congratulations on your win." He glanced at me, extended his hand to shake mine as well, then quickly moved on through the area to view other species. What a moment in time I shall never forget.

CHAPTER 15

A Royal Party

Later that evening, many gathered at the stalls to celebrate the day at the annual exhibitor's party. The Canadians loved to throw parties that would last until the wee hours of the night, and that night was no exception. I enjoyed my time with other breeders, making new friends, and feeling like I was accepted in their group; a feeling I had been longing for all my young life.

Russ Dow, a delightful, charismatic individual, old enough to be my grandfather, was there at the competition with his sheep. Everyone knew and loved him; he was an icon at the show and the highlight of any barn party. It was close to midnight and the party was still very alive with conversation and laughter. Russ was still there, sitting across from me, always keeping an eye on me. Another man, who I knew from showing sheep there, was sitting next to me. I was 30 years younger than him. He seemed to be friendlier towards me than he should have been. I kept ignoring his passes while I sipped on my glass of iced tea. Suddenly, I felt extremely ill and nauseous. I did not understand what was wrong with me. I felt like I was going to pass out. I remember Russ quickly came to my aid, picking me up under his arm, and walking me back to the woman's dormitory where I was staying. He edged me into my cot, covered me with my sleeping bag, and asked another lady there to watch over me. I lay there with the bed spinning, and I could not stop vomiting. I don't remember ever being as ill as I was that night. Early the next morning, Russ came to pick me up and take me to get some breakfast. He told me that the man sitting next to me slipped a pill into my iced tea, hoping to take advantage of me. I thanked God that Russ was my protector that night, protecting me from what could have been the worst night of my life.

One of the final elite events that happened annually at the Royals was the "Sale of the Stars." At that event, all the grand champions were scheduled to be displayed in a live auction. Buyers from all over the world were given an opportunity to purchase the winning sheep to add to their flocks. My friend Russ was the sales manager for the show. I was thrilled when he asked if I would like to be the honorary sheep queen at the Sale of the Stars. My job would be to walk each champion sheep, individually, into the sale block to present them for auction. "Oh, and Prince Phillip is going to be in attendance watching the sale," Russ added. I was speechless and thought I stopped breathing for a few moments. Of course, I said yes!!

The competition was over, but the celebration continued. Russ loved to celebrate his time at the Royals with all his sheep friends. He made close friends with his Canadian Royal whiskey. The evening hours seemed to whisk by and when I looked at my watch, it was after midnight. I walked through our aisle of sheep to check on them before turning in and noticed some of their water buckets needed fresh water. I grabbed a couple of buckets and walked towards the hydrant located down a narrow cement aisle with large circular drains in the floor. As I opened the swing gate to approach the water tap, I noticed a man lying face down, not moving. I dropped the buckets and ran over to the man, kneeling beside him to see if he was okay. His face was over the drain, so I rolled him over. It was Russ! He had an empty bottle of whiskey beside him on the floor and he was drunk as a skunk! I let him know it was me beside him. He tried to speak but I hardly understood what he was saying.

He slurred, "Deb, you gotta get me sober for the sale in the morning. My truck is parked out by the barn. Help me get up and drive me into town for coffee to get me going." I told him I didn't have a driver's license. "Who cares? You'll be fine," he insisted, still slurring his words. There I was with a grown man, practically passed out, soaking wet and cold from laying on the water drain for who knows how long. In a few hours, he was supposed to be dressed in a suit and tie hosting the most prestigious sheep sale in Canada. How was it my responsibility to get him sober quickly?

I struggled to help him up, but once on his feet, he could barely walk. My clothes were wet from him leaning on me as we walked out of the sheep aisle. I was hoping to God that no one saw us. I was trying to protect his image and get him sobered up. After a couple of collapses, I managed to get him to his truck, an old beat-up Chevy that had seen more miles on it than Russ had on him. It had a rusty crumpled bumper that was almost falling off the rear-end. In the back were several bags of grain, bales of hay, a few feeders and buckets covered up with an old weather-torn green canvas. He threw the keys at me and said, "Drive, Deb." I was confident driving on the country roads in Maine, but not in downtown Toronto! I navigated his old rust bucket truck over the lanes, many lefts, rights, and bridges. All the while, I was praying to God no police officer would pull us over. How would I explain how a sixteen-year-old with no license was driving around with a drunk man sitting beside her? We looked like a pair of vagabonds!

After traveling for a few miles, we found an old 24-hour coffee shop that was his go-to while in town. I slid him out of the truck, his arm wrapped around my shoulder as we made our way into the café. I ordered an unlimited amount of coffee and watched him drink as much of it as I could get into him to sober him up. When he came around after a couple of hours, I drove him back to the sheep arena, got him into the men's dormitory, and onto his cot. There were only a few hours left before the

Sale of the Stars, and he assured me he would be fine. After he was settled into his dorm, I went over to my dorm to get a little shut eye myself. In a few hours, the grand finale was scheduled to start.

When I woke up, the first thing I did was check on Russ. When I got to his dorm, he was not in his cot. I went directly to the sheep stalls and there he was, standing upright, washing his face, and shaving over the same water drain I had found him face down in earlier. I watched him make his way back to the dorm. Not long after that he reappeared prim and proper in his fancy gray suit, white pressed shirt, and red Canadian tie ready to get the Sale of Stars rolling. He appeared to have had a perfect night's sleep! The sale started on time with hundreds of spectators in attendance, including Prince Phillip. I gracefully walked the grand champions around the sale ring so potential buyers could view and bid on them. The auctioneer spoke about each sheep's pedigree, then with that glorious twang and speed of auctioneers, sold each one.

Lost in the event's grandeur, time had lapsed so quickly I had not realized I was supposed to be leaving for the airport to catch my return flight. Russ had made arrangements with a friend to get me to the airport. I quickly packed my suitcase, readying for the ride back. Russ met me at the dormitory and said anxiously "We have a problem. Your ride is not here yet." Time was of the essence, and I needed to leave immediately, or I would miss my flight. The panic was palpable for both of us. Just then, around the corner came a stunningly beautiful lady dressed to the nines, wearing a satin sash over her shoulder that read "Finland." She was tall, with beautiful long blonde hair, perfect makeup, wearing a stunning dress, and high heels to finish the polished look. She looked exactly as you would expect a beauty contest winner to look. She was there as an ambassador from the Department of Agriculture, representing her country. Accompanying her was a Canadian Mountie guard, dressed in their beautiful red uniform with the top high fuzzy black hat strapped under his chin. He looked very official as her security escort, and he knew Russ as well. Everyone knew Russ. He seemed a bit stressed. "Russ, Karolina needs a ride to the airport straightaway. Our driver did not show up, can you help?" You could see the anxiety written all over Russ' face.

"God help me," Russ said. "I have two queens who need a ride to the airport!"

Russ could not drive us because it was his responsibility to finish the paperwork involved cashing out buyers from the sale. Looking around frantically, Russ saw a few feet away, a very gruff-looking elderly gentleman with a long weathered gray beard, with hair almost as long. He had a couple of brown teeth showing when he smiled, wearing tattered old clothing. He looked like he hadn't changed or washed his clothes in some time. He had just delivered three male goats to another breeder outside at the docks. Russ turned to him and said, "Samson, would you be able to give these ladies a ride over to the airport? They need to leave right now, or they will both miss their flights.

Samson agreed but noted, "I got no seats in the van, they're gonna have to ride in the back."

At that point, anything with wheels was what we needed. Karolina and I hurried outside to his van which was parked right along the building. It was a rust-crusted old white van with dents everywhere. He swung open the back doors for us to climb in, and the putrid stench of male bucks overpowered us. There was a scant scattering of sawdust on the floor, dusted with a few manure pebbles here and there and a couple of yellow urine puddles in the corners. Samson said, "Oh hell. I think I have a tarp up front, let me get that and throw it down for you." When he flung open the front side door, it creaked from being so rusty. I thought it was going to fall off its hinges. Samson grabbed an oversized heavy green, musty army canvas tarp and spread it out on the floor of the van. "You'll have a nice clean place to sit now," he boasted. Karolina and I threw our suitcases in, climbed into the van and sat down as best we could. We looked at each other as if to say, "Is this really happening?" We tried to breathe through the heavy stench of urine, plus "the other ingredients." Suddenly, we both burst out laughing! Enveloped in the putrid aroma, we sat cross-legged in the goat van at the mercy of a stranger who had to get us to the airport. We went from high-exposure queens who were just under the spotlight amongst royalty, to a manure, urine ridden putrid goat van in under an hour! How great life was! We both knew the horrid aroma was going to cling to our clothing and started thinking ahead of how we were going to explain the smell while sitting on our plane ride home.

Samson drove so fast that Karolina and I lost our balance several times and fell over sideways. We tried to hang on to each other for dear life, hoping the canvas would stay in place so we would not roll onto what was underneath! Karolina's high heels flew off her feet as we rolled around the van, hanging on for dear life.

When we reached our destination, Samson opened the back doors of the van and assisted Karolina out first. She readjusted her sash, smoothed her disheveled hair, fixed her dress, and slipped her high heels back on. I hopped out behind her. We both hugged Samson, thanking him for the ride. In that short ride to the airport, two queens from a world away formed an unforgettable bond. We hugged each other, and laughed until we cried. When we said goodbye, we were still giggling as we turned away to hurry to our respective gates. Imagine the thoughts of the people pulling up behind the van at the gate, seeing two queens bailing out of a rusty old goat van. I do not think they could ever guess!

Soon after returning home, I received an exquisite handwritten letter from Mrs. Gartshore. I treasured her eloquent words, thanking me for all I did for them. In the last sentence of her letter, she expressed that she felt I had a special gift with sheep that I should be proud of. The letter touched the deepest part of my soul and inspired me to keep chasing my dream of becoming a professional shepherd. It was a letter I cherished, but my mother threw it away.

That unforgettable week in Toronto will always be etched in my mind as one of the greatest experiences of my life.

CHAPTER 16

The Green Swamp Monster

Spending my summers traveling to the various fairs to show my sheep had many fun moments. During the 70s, I attended the Lewiston Fair, a smaller event held in conjunction with the home of the racehorses from the Lewiston Racetrack. The sheep barn was in the far corner of the fairgrounds next to a major set of railroad tracks. There was a small pathway leading to an old broken gate behind the barn where some locals used to sneak through to avoid paying admission. Long thunderous trains passed through a few times a day so loudly you could not hear yourself think. When the train went flying by, the barns shook, but the sheep never seemed to mind it. The sheep competition at Lewiston, a small county fair with low attendance, wasn't highly regarded, but we participated anyway to have a shot at winning prize money. The event attracted local sheep farmers who rarely show on the regular circuit. There was a keen lack of competition and quality of entrants. Some farmers, hoping to earn a few dollars, hauled in their backyard sheep.

One afternoon, I had one of my show sheep on the grooming stand, preparing it for the show, which was going to be held the next day. I had trimmed the fleece and was preparing to return it to its pen. I was about to put a show blanket on to keep it clean when a dilapidated rust bucket of an old truck pulled up with five dirty wooly sheep in the back. The sheep were all sticking their heads out through the wooden panel gates on the bed of the truck. They were pushing and shoving each other like they wanted to get out of that truck in a hurry. Show sheep typically have less than two inches of snow-white fleece. The sheep in the back of that truck looked like they had just been pulled out of a pasture with no show preparation done to them at all! They had long matted fleeces, at least five inches long, full of burdocks (like round thorn weeds), tangled throughout their fleece. Gobs of dried manure tags hung from their behinds like Christmas tree bulbs, swinging back and forth as they moved. The long wool dangled from their eyebrows and you could barely see their faces. I thought to myself, "How is this man ever going to get them ready for the show tomorrow?"

A thin, elderly man slid out of the cab of the truck and slammed the door which was so dented it did not close completely. He had long stringy, greasy hair and a straggly beard that hung so low it touched his chest. With a long cigarette hanging from his mouth he said, "Hey, where do the sheep go?" I pointed to some empty pens that were still available in the barn. "Well, I ain't never been to a show before and my sheep never left the farm either 'til today. I got no clue 'bout these things," he admitted.

"No worries, we will help you out. My name is Deb."

"Okay. Thanks. My name is Lester." He hopped back in his old clunker of a truck. It backfired twice, sounding like a cannon, as he drove over to the barn area to offload his sheep. Instead of holding the sheep one at a time and leading them off individually, Lester swung open the rear gate of the truck. When the sheep eyed freedom, five of them took a long leap off the truck and headed for the carnival, which was several hundred feet away from the barns. They were running so fast that they were out of sight in no time. What a chaotic situation!

There were some fair-goers who were watching the spectacle and helped chase them down. They did not know that the worst thing you can do to sheep running loose is to chase them down. The more you chase them, the further they will run. They did not stay together in a group, which made it even more difficult to catch them. I immediately took my ewe off the grooming stand so I could go help with the rodeo. A few other seasoned sheep exhibitors volunteered to catch the wild beasts. There were so many people chasing them, they split up. I saw one of them jump on the moving merry-go-round and take a spin around while people were screaming as if there were killer sheep on the loose. Another one dove about one hundred feet away, under the Ferris wheel, while the other three headed towards the racetrack that was quite a distance away.

The commotion drew the attention of the fair officials who rounded up as many golf carts as they could to join the chase. It was pure pandemonium! I was able to grab the one sheep that jumped on the merry-go-round after it came around for the second time. It took all the strength I had to hold onto it while it snorted at me. Another sheep exhibitor grabbed the one from under the Ferris wheel. Over thirty minutes later, some horsemen cornered the other three in a horse stall. Everyone was out of breath, including the sheep.

The sheep had not been trained to lead on a halter, so the trek back to the barn was a long one. They all ended up being carried by bystanders and put into the sheep pens. I wondered how Lester was going to show his sheep the next day, because he would have to keep them still in the show ring. That afternoon, he did not even try to get any of them ready for the show. Lester said, "Ahh--I will just haul 'em in the ring and see how they do." Something told me we were in for an experience. The next morning, when the show started with the classes, everything was going smoothly until it was Lester's time to bring his sheep into the show ring for judging. As he walked into the pen to catch one, they were all so wild they kept jumping over each other until they were two deep on top of one another to avoid being caught. He finally caught one, but since it was not used to being handled, it did not walk with him. Lester picked it up and carried it, with its legs flailing in every direction, to the show ring. When he got to the middle of the ring, he plunked it down in front of the judge as if it were a crate of cabbage! You could tell the judge was astounded at the appearance of the sheep in front of him. When the judge approached it to do a quick examination, the sheep snorted like a mad bull, and sprang out of Lester's arms in one huge leap. The second session of the rodeo had begun as the sheep headed towards the back gate near the railroad tracks. We were all concerned that a train might come along.

A couple of men tried to stop it, but it was so strong and wild, it flew past both of them. The show was temporarily stopped as people ran after it. I was yelling for them to not chase it, but it was too late! Two teen boys, who were far ahead of me, were chasing it as fast as they could run. The longer they ran after it, the further the sheep went. After chasing it about a ½ mile down the track, the sheep suddenly bolted to the left and ran down a steep embankment. At the bottom of the embankment was a deep algae-infested swamp matted with swamp weeds crisscrossing in every direction over the green murky water. Just as I thought it might, the sheep took one long leap into a deep part of the vile swamp and tried to swim away.

With the water absorbing into the thick, heavy fleece, the weight of the water was going to pull it down quickly. Thankfully, they caught it, dragged it out of the swamp, and back onto the bank after much pulling and pushing to get it to cooperate. The sheep was completely covered from head to tail in thick, dark green, slimy algae with long stringy swamp weeds hanging off it. Before it went swimming, it weighed approximately 150 pounds, but after the water adventure, the weight was doubled. It resembled a swamp monster from a horror movie and was indistinguishable as a sheep!

It was too exhausted and heavy from the weight of the water to walk on its own. The two boys locked arms and carried it, having to stop and rest along the way. Because of the sheer weight of the sheep, it took over an hour to get the beast back to the sheep barn. The boys, soaking wet and covered in swamp slime, were smiling like heroes. Once everyone caught their breath again, the show resumed. Rather than risk another getaway, the judge volunteered to walk over to the pens where the rest of Lester's sheep were to examine them there. After the show, Lester sat quietly on a bale of hay near the sheep pen, reminiscing about the day. He looked up at me and said, "Guess I probably should've raised racehorses!"

When it was time for Lester to leave, everyone in the barn stepped forward to assist in getting his sheep loaded onto his truck. No one wanted to risk another rodeo. We tied the gate shut securely, and as Lester slipped into his truck to return home, he leaned out the window and with his toothless smile said "See you all next year!"

CHAPTER 17

Risky Business

The Lewiston Fair offered many other memorable adventures. During my 4-H years, I missed a great deal of school because I was always on the road earning money for the farm. I genuinely loved my fair life. I had always loved horses and since their stalls were near the sheep barn, I always found time to sneak over to kiss the noses of the horses looking out from their stalls watching me work. I could not resist running my cheeks over their velvet noses and pushing my face deep into the hair on their necks and shoulders. Inhaling their musty horse smell was magical and therapeutic for me.

The 4-H sheep show usually attracted fierce competition with beautiful awards for the winners. Each year the champion showmen were awarded large engraved Paul Revere silver bowls. They were a treasure, but difficult to win. I had won several of the engraved silver bowls over the years and had remained undefeated in that competition. The superintendent who oversaw the competition was Paul Dowell. He was very personable and fun to be around, and I looked forward to seeing him each year. While putting the finishing touches on my favorite sheep getting her ready for the contest, I saw Paul driving towards me on a golf cart. He was looking somewhat panicked. "Deb, I need a huge favor from you," he said. "The local newspaper reporter is in my office needing a photo and story regarding the livestock shows to print in tonight's paper to promote the fair. Can you help?" I was eager and willing to help him out anyway I could.

"What can I do?" I asked.

"Well, in my career, I have never done this. You've won the Paul Revere bowl every year for as long as I can remember. How about I bring the reporter up to the barn and let him take a picture of you holding it as this year's winner? If you lose, I'll probably lose my job, but I have confidence in you."

I was honored that he showed so much faith in me, but I felt pressure. Not wanting to let him down since he asked me for a favor, I obliged. "I'll be right back," he said hopping back on his golf cart to get the reporter. A few minutes later, they drove up and Paul walked towards me carrying the beautiful bowl. He passed it to me to hold as the reporter clicked a photo of me, smiling. After the photo, I passed it back to Paul to return to the livestock office for safekeeping until the official competition the next day. The reporter thanked us for our time, quickly jumped in his car and disappeared out of sight.

Thoughts raced through my mind. *What if I do not win? What will Paul say? How will he feel? He has held this position of livestock superintendent for over thirty years. He is now in jeopardy of losing his job if I cannot win this thing tomorrow.* I had never been asked to do anything like that before and I was feeling immense pressure. I took pride in never letting anyone down and I could not let my friend Paul down. I had already put the perfecting touches on my ewe, Corvette. She was ready for the morning. However, with the pressure of the challenge ahead of me, I planned to spend more time on her the next morning. I felt the need to ensure she would stand out amongst all the competitors—she had to. I had to.

The competition was set to start at nine that morning. I jumped out of my sleeping bag at 5:00 a.m. to bring Corvette out of her pen and polish her fitting job one more time. So much was at stake. I went over every inch of her body, making sure she was perfectly clean, carding her fleece, and hand trimming it with my shears until it was perfect white velvet. I rubbed white cornstarch on her knees and ears to give them a snow-white appearance. I cleaned the inside of her ears with Q-tips so they too were spotless. I even scrubbed her hooves with hot soapy water with an old used toothbrush. They shined like a pair of new shoes. I made every effort I could dig up for us to come in first. The show began at 9:00 A.M. sharp with the prestigious fitting and showmanship class first. There were close to thirty entrants, which was a record. The judge examined our sheep meticulously while demanding top performance of our sheep handling. He asked tough questions regarding our knowledge of our sheep project. This pressure-filled grueling workout lasted over an hour. With every passing moment, I reminded myself of the pressure I was under to win. Failure simply was not an option. Just before I entered the show ring, I saw Paul sitting in the audience watching intently during the entire class. I could only imagine what must have been going through his mind, but I could not make eye contact with him. Once you are in the show ring showing your sheep, you are not allowed to look at the spectators or you lose points from the judge. If you were caught looking at anything else other than your sheep or the judge, points were taken away. I was sweating from all the physical and mental effort I was putting forth, praying that Corvette would hang in there with me and behave. Sure enough, after a grueling hour of digging deep into my skills, I was able to win. I saw Paul walking into the show ring carrying the coveted silver bowl. He passed it to me, shaking my sweaty hand for the win in front of the spectator crowd as he winked and whispered "I knew you would do it, Deb."

I took a stroll over to the newspaper stand at the entrance gate not far away to get a copy of the daily paper. There was my large photo on the front cover of the paper with a caption underneath that read: "The first day of the fair opens with a winner." I was that winner.

CHAPTER 18
The Art Show

I was enrolled in the art program my senior year in high school. I was very creative and taught myself the art of scratch-boarding after watching another student do it. Scratch-boarding is a way to create an image using a special board with a black surface layer and a white layer below. The resulting image is a series of light lines against a dark background. I concentrated on an elevated level of detail in them and was especially interested in drawing wildlife.

I spent hours drawing beautiful scenes and was honored that one of my designs was used on the front cover of the senior yearbook that year. As graduation approached, we were gearing up for an exciting art show in the gymnasium. The public was invited to admire our year-end creations.

My mother spent a lot of her time creating oil paintings, mostly of ocean scenes. Some were indeed, quite beautiful. She never entered them into competition but just hung them around the house. My entry was due at school the next day, and I was feeling hopeful and excited to see how my piece would do. As I was carefully wrapping my picture for transportation, my mother approached and told me I was not to take my picture. I was going to take *her* most recent oil painting of an ocean scene. "I want this entered. It will be a good way for me to get recognition for it," she coldly said. "You tell them you painted it," she instructed, and tossed my entry away. I felt an overwhelming feeling of disappointment and sadness that she was taking my opportunity away from me. The feeling of terror overtook me as I realized she was expecting me to lie to my teacher. After I dried my tears from disappointment, she had me wrap her large painting that was four times the size of my art piece, in protective paper. I knew my teacher, Mrs. Tate, who was a very accomplished artist herself, would intuitively know the painting was not my work. It was a far better quality than I could ever do. I was horrified and ashamed to take it to school as my entry. My mother had subjected me to the most shamefully awkward position I could have found myself in. I was nauseated as I walked into the art room to submit my mother's piece of work. I felt weak in my knees as I set it on the teacher's table. She looked at me in total disbelief. I could feel my soul melting into a deep state of shame. She asked, "Deb, did you do this work?" I burst into tears because I could not lie to her, but if I disobeyed my mother, the consequences would be even worse.

In a split-second decision, I decided my character was more important than any anticipated beating, so I shamefully replied, "No, Mrs. Tate." In her wisdom, I think she suspected my home situation. To protect me, she elected to let my mother think her painting was entered in the show. She placed it in a closet in her office until the show was over. I was grateful for her grace to me, but as a consequence for my action, I was disqualified from the art show. My heart sank and tears flowed, but I understood her decision to do the right thing. Once again, I was paying the price for another one of my mother's actions.

The next day I had to walk through the gymnasium to look at all the entrants beautifully displayed under spotlights. I saw the beautiful blue rosettes awarded to the winners hanging on their art pieces. My heart ached as I so badly wanted one of those hanging on my work, but I was denied the chance. Again, I learned about another piece of my mother. As far as she knew, her art was entered but won nothing. She did not attend the art show, and I knew she would not have gone even if my submission had been there.

CHAPTER 19

Wounded in Battle

After graduation, we were on our fourth week out on the road traveling with my parents and competing with our sheep in multiple competitions throughout New England. The higher we placed in the competitions, the more we earned. Each fair we competed in had two divisions. The first division was the "open show," which was open to exhibitors of any age. The second was the 4-H division, which only allowed 4-H club members under the age of nineteen to compete. Because each fair had two categories that we could compete in, we could earn double prize money. Most farms competed with eight sheep, but we traveled with forty-five to earn as much money as possible. Keeping the sheep all groomed was a full-time job for me. The better they looked, the greater the chance of moving up to the top placings. I spent all my days, from morning until after dark, fitting my group of "show string" sheep. It required a strong work ethic and highly detailed skills that took me many years to master. Standing on my feet for hours was grueling and demanding, but I mastered my craft just as any artist masters theirs. My father rarely assisted with the fitting; he and my mother would just sit and watch me.

The other 4-H members who showed along with me in sheep, horses, and cattle categories could keep their prize money to contribute to their college funds, but whatever prize money I earned went directly to the farm. I was forbidden to even think about attending college, so that was never an option for me. There was always intense pressure from my parents for me to win because of the higher payouts. It was never about "go have fun and win some blue ribbons." Instead, it was "you win or else."

We had just traveled from one fair, and I had the sheep settled into their new home for the week's competition. My father decided I needed to drive home to the farm to pick up a few supplies he needed. It was a one-hundred-mile round trip for me that evening. The 4-H sheep competition was scheduled to start the next morning at 8:00 a.m., so I had little time to waste. I was feeling tired, so I took my friend Ron, who also showed sheep, with me for the trip back to the farm. We made it home, checked the sheep in their summer pastures, loaded up the supplies I was to retrieve, and prepared to head back to the fair. It was late, and I was not a fan of driving at night, so Ron offered to drive.

We were halfway back to the fair and stopped at a red light. Ron was signaling to make a left turn and when the light turned green, we proceeded. Suddenly, I saw bright headlights coming right at me at a high rate of speed, blinding me. I knew at that moment we were going to be hit. The next thing I remember was looking down and seeing the back seat of the car almost touching the dashboard in front of me. I was crumpled up in the front right corner of the dashboard with parts of the car wrapped around me. I felt sharp pains in my head and warm blood running down my face, saturating my blouse. I looked over and saw Ron pull himself out of the car, uninjured. There was a popular twenty-four-hour restaurant directly across the road. People were running out of the restaurant towards our scene to help. It was a blur of police and ambulance sirens with red and blue lights flashing everywhere. A kind soft-spoken firefighter pulled me out of the mangled carnage and laid me on a stretcher. My knee was hurting so bad, I was afraid I had a broken leg. "I have to show my sheep in the morning," I told the paramedic, panicking about not being able to make it back to the fair.

The woman who was a passenger of the vehicle that hit us was also on a stretcher, bleeding profusely from her face. Her lower lip was cut so severely that it was dangling below her chin. Suddenly, the driver of the car that hit us came around the corner of the ambulance, appearing extremely agitated. He tried to jump into the ambulance that was about to transport me to the hospital. He thought I was the driver and screamed at me, threatening to beat me up for hitting them and hurting his wife. The police officers strong-armed him and pulled him down to the pavement while another officer arrested and handcuffed him. The police found a half-empty, half gallon of vodka in the front seat of his car. At the moment of impact, his wife had been sipping vodka from her glass, and her lower lip was shredded when the glass shattered. I was later informed it was not their first accident because of intoxication while driving.

The ambulance door slammed shut and we made the twenty-five-mile ride to the hospital; the same one I was born in. They examined me in the emergency room, pulling shards of glass out of the side of my head and stitching half of my left ear back on. At the moment of impact, my head was driven through the windshield, leaving a hole. Long strands of my blonde hair covered in blood were still hanging webbed through the shattered glass. The car was completely totaled. Had I not been wearing my seatbelt, the police officers stated that I probably would not have survived. God granted me the one chance in a million that night. After the x-ray of my knees, it was determined that there were no broken bones. I was sutured up, my head wrapped several times around with thick white gauze, and I was given instructions to rest quietly for the next few days. The pressure of the gauze made my head feel better. Ron telephoned my parents back at the fair to inform them what happened and let them know they needed to come pick us up at the hospital. After a long wait, they finally showed up to take us back to the fair. Neither of my parents asked if I was okay, nor did they request to speak to the attending doctor. Instead, the first words out of my father's mouth were, "You need to show first thing in the morning."

We made the return trip back to the fairgrounds and into the camper trailer that we lived in week to week while traveling the show circuit. It was about two in the morning and I was very sleepy and hurting. I laid myself down on the couch to quietly rest for a few brief hours. Before I knew it, my mother was shaking me to get up and ready to show. She walked me by my arm to the tiny narrow bathroom and started to unwrap the gauze bandage that was to stay on my head for a couple more days. "You can't wear that thing in the show ring," she snarled. She had me kneel in front of the bathtub with my head over the edge. With the hosed showerhead, she rinsed the dried blood off my head with chilly water. I could hear the gobs of tiny pieces of glass falling from my long hair onto the tub and floor. The cuts that had been stitched were very sore and surely were not supposed to be getting wet. My mother was determined to wash away any evidence that I had been hurt. It was painful, but her priority was to get me in the show ring to earn them money.

Lucky for me, my favorite Dorset ewe, Corvette, was highly trained due to the countless hours we had spent together. She was always gentle whenever I worked with her. I was able to get her to jump on the fitting stand for a few minutes before the competition. I washed her face, smoothed her fleece with my hand shears, and scrubbed her hooves clean along with other last-minute preps. I whispered in her soft white ear "I need your help today friend." I know she understood; she had never let me down.

Corvette and I entered the show facing intense competition that morning. Twenty other competitors lined up beside us, all vying for the big win. The first class shown was based solely on which exhibitor did the best overall job of fitting and presenting their sheep to its highest potential to the judge. The judge also asked each competitor specific questions about their sheep to determine the depth of their knowledge. It was such a large class that we had been competing for over an hour— double the normal time required. I had a pounding headache, and my knees were aching from the accident, but I kept pushing forward. I occasionally leaned into Corvette to help keep my balance. The skill levels of the class were so intense, the judge determined a tie-breaking move would be required. He instructed each competitor to trade sheep with another competitor to determine if we could present someone else's animal as well or better than their owner. My Corvette was so experienced with the drills from being in so many previous shows, she knew the routine. When it was time to trade her off to another competitor, she misbehaved immediately. She stood up in the air on her rear legs, threw her head around, and swung her body in circles, refusing to stand still no matter how hard the new handler tried. She made it clear with loud "baa's" that she did not want anyone else handling her except me.

It was always an intense showdown to break a tie, but I had an ace in my pocket with Corvette. "The Grand Champion Showman" title was always my favorite class because it was not based on the quality of the animal. It was based on the bond between sheep and handler and how well you both present your skills under pressure. Corvette and I won that title, and once the entire show concluded, four hours later, Corvette won the "Best in Show" award for her qualities over all the other breeds of sheep that day. With over two hundred other sheep in competition, we made it through the show together with determination and grit. That same day I showed twenty other sheep in their breed classes to earn a good $400 paycheck for the farm.

The skills I was learning were instrumental building blocks in my junior years that I could carry with me into my career as a shepherdess. I hoped to one day be able to compete at the U.S. National level, which would require masterfully refined fitting and showmanship skills. No one else ever knew what happened to me less than twelve hours before the competition. They had no clue how remarkably close I came to not being able to show that day—or any other day ever again.

Debby Jo and Corvette 1972

CHAPTER 20
Never Give Up

That October, a few months later, our last show of the year culminated at the state fair, which was the second largest show in New England. Thousands of livestock, comprised of dairy and beef cattle, horses, swine, sheep, goats, poultry, rabbits, and llamas, were there to compete. Over four hundred high quality sheep that had been preparing for the show all summer were entered. I knew the competition would require every ounce of skill I could muster. I spent many hours fitting my sheep each day leading up to the competition, so they looked like white velvet.

I had moved up to the senior division and would compete against older members who were highly polished and experienced. The judge was a professor of animal science at a highly respected college in Connecticut. With a lifetime of judging experience, he was a very thorough but tough judge with high expectations. Feeling well prepared, my heart was racing with excitement as I tried to keep my focus on the job at hand. The show arena bleachers were packed full of spectators; not an empty seat to be found. The warm bright spotlights were shining down on the fresh pine-smelling sawdust in the show ring as the anticipation grew. My class was lined up outside of the arena waiting for the show announcer to call us in. I looked over my shoulder and saw a line so long I could not see the end. It was a large class and would be a tough one to win.

When the announcement came over the loudspeakers, "All senior members, please enter the ring at this time," I whispered in Corvette's ear, "Today is our day, friend. Let's go." I held her beautiful head high as we gracefully entered the ring, taking our place in the lineup. I could hear the spectators all whispering and pointing to their favorites. It was a showdown. As normal protocol, we were all put through our paces. We walked around the show ring in large circles, leading our sheep slow and steady. We would stop when instructed by the judge to see who could pose their sheep the fastest and most accurately to make our sheep look its best. The judge came to each one of us asking pertinent questions regarding our knowledge of our sheep, such as feeding and health-related questions regarding their care. He then motioned for us to line up our animal's head to tail on a side view for him to make his final determination of placings. The process lasted over an hour, which is a long time to keep an animal alert, still, and in control. The judge then motioned to a girl from Massachusetts, who I had never competed against, to take a spot in the first-place position. He then motioned to Corvette and me to place second. He continued placing the remaining contestants down to twenty spots. Space was limited, so the rest of the class was dismissed.

I was proud that Corvette and I placed well, but in my heart, I wanted that first-place win. I continued showing her off, holding her head high, keeping her ears perked forward, with all four legs placed squarely underneath her to give the important look of balance. The judge walked down the line one more time before walking to the announcer's table. Picking up his microphone, he addressed the spectators to let them know why he placed everyone in their respective placing. As he gave his speech, the girl in the first place slot started laughing and motioning to the crowd with a thumbs up. She was not paying attention and let her sheep turn sideways, out of position. She assumed the competition was over and was just waiting for the beautiful trophy to be passed to her. The judge briefly spoke about her and her sheep, then he moved to my position to speak about my performance and why I was in second place. I continued to show Corvette, making sure she looked her best. Suddenly, the judge announced, "This young lady, in second place, is going to be my winner today because she never gave up, nor stopped showing her sheep, even though she had not won the class." He continued his remarks by saying, "The young lady in first place immediately stopped showing her sheep after she assumed she won the class. Therefore, would you two please swap positions?" He then delivered a stern lecture. "You should never stop showing your animal until you have exited the show ring." The young lady from Massachusetts angrily pushed her sheep out of the ring, sputtering negative comments towards the judge as she left in a cloud of dust.

Later that afternoon, the president of the fair appeared at my stalls in the barn and congratulated me on my win. He announced that the ABC television show, "Good Morning America" was at the fairgrounds with a film crew requesting to interview some outstanding fair exhibitors. He told me that I was his choice to represent the sheep department. "Would you like to be on TV?" he asked.

"I would be honored to!" was my joyful reply.

He asked me to bring Corvette to the interview at the grandstand where the TV crew was setting up their cameras for the live show. Corvette and I walked through the crowds heading towards another thrill of a lifetime. The hosts asked many questions about my sheep and my experiences competing. They thought Corvette was the prettiest sheep they had ever seen. As they stroked her beautiful face, I was beaming with pride. She and I completed our show season with such a perfect ending. The lesson of perseverance, "never give up," was the most significant takeaway from that day. It would guide me in the years to come.

CHAPTER 21
Graduation Celebration

My high school graduation was fast approaching, and my sights were set on graduating. Since my father never progressed beyond eighth grade, an education for me and my sister was not his priority. My parents discredited those who attended college and I was forbidden to even mention the word. As my classmates relished the grandeur of the pre-graduation ceremonies, I could not stay after school for any of the festivities. My classmates and their families attended the ceremonies, taking lots of photos for such a special occasion, but I was required to be home doing chores.

When graduation night arrived, the seniors were instructed to meet outside the gymnasium thirty minutes early to have a class photo taken. When it was time to leave for the ceremony, I was very anxious because my parents considered the graduation ceremony to be a chore, not a celebration. We did not leave the farm in time for me to be there for the group photo, and I was so disappointed. I was also afraid that I would be late for my graduation.

I arrived at the ceremony with barely enough time to slip in line and march with my classmates. I was overjoyed when I was invited to attend the graduation party. The party would be at the local lake. Being invited made me feel like I was finally being accepted as one of them. As I crossed the stage, received my diploma, and marched out of the gymnasium door, I was met by my best friend Wanda. She was also a farm girl, whom I adored. She threw her arms around me, and we hugged as if we would not see each other again for years. My father immediately stepped in, grabbed my arm, and escorted me to his truck. "You're not going to any graduation party, " he said sternly. "Now you are going to work!" We drove straight back to the farm as if it were just another day. There was no party for me, no card, no cake, nothing.

On that beautiful warm June evening with a full moon shining on the farm pond, I sat alone, locked in my room for the rest of the night. Eyes filled with tears I imagined what it must have been like to be at the lake party. As I gazed through my gray window, I thought, *There must be a better life out there for me, and I need to find it.*

After graduation, I continued working extremely hard in the sawmill day after day. I began preparing for the upcoming travel season with the sheep. One of the first shows we attended was a small fair with very light competition, but my father said, "It will be a paycheck." I spent many hours preparing the sheep to look their absolute best, as always. When the show day arrived, we earned a good paycheck for the farm. That evening, some of the other livestock kids invited me to walk around with them and take in the sights to relax. Shockingly, my father allowed me to go with the other teenagers! As I left, he shouted, "You be back at the camper by 10:30!"

I had a grand time strolling around the carnival absorbing all the bright colors of the whirling rides and the smells of popcorn and cotton candy. I did not have a watch, so I asked one girl for the time. "It's 10:10," she reported. I said goodnight to everyone, telling them I had to return to my camper, and left. It was a five-minute walk back to the camper. I knew I had time to do one last check on the sheep before bedtime. I noticed that some of their water buckets needed to be refreshed, so I refilled them with fresh water. I gave each pen of sheep a little fresh hay to munch on for a snack for the evening to ensure they were content. Suddenly, I saw a large black shadow appear from behind me. It was my father.

Pointing his bony finger in my face, he screamed, "You are in big trouble! It is almost 10:30 and you are not in the camper!" He could see that I was taking care of the sheep, but that did not matter to him. He grabbed both of my long braids of hair in one fist and dragged me down through the sheep barn area where my friends had gathered. With my feet barely touching the ground, he dragged me past the cattle barn, screaming at the top of his lungs at me for being "no good for anything." When we arrived at the camper, he forcefully swung open the camper door, stepping up in it first. He turned around with my braids still in his fist, and yanked me inside. He flung me over to the bunk bed like a rag doll, and took those same weathered bony hands I had absorbed so many times and slapped me hard multiple times in my face. That time, he did not even provide me with a handkerchief for my bloody nose. I was mortified at the thought of my friends witnessing what had just happened to me.

The next day, early in the afternoon, I was visiting with a friend who lived near the fairgrounds. He was a nice young man who was a couple of years older than me, and every year when we were in town for the fair, we hung out. The two of us were in the barn talking, laughing, and passing time, as teenagers do, when suddenly my mother appeared around the corner of the barn. In a shrill voice advancing quickly towards me, she yelled, "What do you think you are doing?" I was not doing anything out of the ordinary, so I was not sure how to answer her. Suddenly, just as my father had done the night before, she grabbed my braids and dragged me away from my friend. I was absolutely humiliated.

She took me down the same path that my father had dragged me through the night before. Through the sheep barn, and through a cattle barn, with everyone witnessing her demoralizing me. She screamed the entire trip, "You are a useless tramp!" My legs staggered along the way from her force. She flung me into a lawn chair, and for the rest of the afternoon, in the sweltering summer sun, at 17 years old, I was in "time out" for "talking to boys." I sat there and sobbed. I loathed my parents for the humiliation and injustice they were putting me through.

CHAPTER 22

When You Know, You Know

At the end of the season, attending the last fair of the year, I caught up with my friend, Lee, who was also showcasing her sheep in the competition. Lee was a very warm and kind person who I had known for most of my teen years. I always looked up to her. I was standing at my sheep pen, answering questions from spectators, when Lee appeared from the back of the crowd holding the arm of a tall, handsome young man. She introduced him to me as her good friend, Cliff.

I was captivated by his warm shy smile, his bright blue eyes, and curly blonde hair. I didn't know what to talk to him about, so I jumped in the pen with my sheep and proudly showed them to him. He seemed quite interested, and during our conversation, his laughs came easily. He was a herdsman for a large horse farm and invited me over to the horse barn where his horses were stalled. His horses had competed all over New England and had participated in many parades. His Belgians were a beautiful butterscotch blonde color, with white manes and stunning white blazes running down their foreheads. In the competitions, they competed with a six-horse hitch, similar to the Budweiser hitch. Cliff talked proudly about his horses, and introduced me to his favorite horse, King. King was a stallion they used for breeding and was the lead on their hitch. His face beamed with pride as he told me he was the owner of King.

We hit it off instantly, both having a common interest in livestock. It has been said that you have a gut feeling when you meet the right person. Well, I knew he was "the one." When I returned home the next day, I was so excited about meeting Cliff, I ran to my neighbor's house and told her, "I just met the man I'm going to marry one day!"

During the next few months, I became very fond of Cliff. Although he lived eighty miles away, he came to visit me often. My father could see we were serious about each other and it didn't take long before he began treating Cliff badly. One day after Cliff had just left from a visit, my father cornered me against the kitchen wall with his shoulder. He pointed his finger just inches from my eyes and screamed "You either get rid of him, or I will." I knew he meant it, and in that moment, I decided enough was enough.

I grabbed two black plastic garbage bags, raced upstairs to my room and proceeded to feverishly throw a few handfuls of clothes into one bag. I grabbed a glass jar that contained $8 in pennies and threw it in the bag. My heart was racing at full speed from fear. Five years earlier, my sister had made her getaway. She was too frightened to face my parents, so she left in the dark while they were away for a weekend. When they discovered she had left, my mother screamed at me, "I will shoot you if I ever hear of you communicating with your sister again." I knew she had a pistol in her bedroom, so I believed her.

With a few clothes and my pennies in the first bag, I put some of my prized possessions in the second bag. A special bible Momma Jo had given me and a few other special pictures I had of my sheep were among those prized possessions. The first bag was heavy, so I flew down the narrow staircase with the heavy bag of clothes and pennies and intended to return for the second bag. As I approached the front door, my mother and my father both stood puffed up in front of me. "What the hell do you think you are doing?" my father screamed.

With tremors in my voice and my heart pounding, I said "I am leaving!"

"All I did was raise two daughters that are useless bitches!" my mother snarled and stormed off to another room.

My father shouted to her, "Take Nell and lock her in our bedroom so she doesn't take her."

He pounded his huge fist on the kitchen table in his rage so hard that the dishes shattered into pieces. I was terrified that I would receive the next blow. In a moment of desperation, I felt like darkness would completely encompass me if I did not make my move immediately.

I quickly slipped out the door carrying the clothes and pennies and set them on the front seat of my old truck. I briefly considered a return trip back upstairs to retrieve the second bag containing my priceless items. My mother, with a smirk on her face, slammed the front door shut. She slid the deadbolt into place, locking me out. There was no going back. All of a sudden, my father lunged from around the back of the house and aggressively approached me with his fist clinched in the air. He seemed to be twice the size that he normally was. I was sure he was going to unleash his fury on me, and I prepared myself for a hard blow. He puffed his shoulders high. With his dark piercing eyes permeating me, screamed, inches from my face, "You will never be anything, or ever raise a sheep without me!" He then spit a mouthful of the white bubbling saliva running out of the corner of his mouth, directly on my face. As the saliva dribbled down my cheeks he continued to scream at me. "I should just kick you to the ground now and finish you!" I shook uncontrollably as the adrenaline rushed fiercely through my body. I knew I could never allow him another chance to inflict his terror on me. Never again! I was having difficulty breathing and could not speak. I did not respond, but quickly jumped in my truck, locked the door, and pulled out of the driveway. I faded out of his sight, carrying my half bag of clothes and a few pennies. Along with my few possessions, I carried the physical and emotional scars that had been inflicted by my parents over my lifetime, while also reflecting I never heard the words during those years of "I love you" from them. I had no idea where I was headed, but I had faith in myself that I would survive, no matter what. As I drove away, I did not shed a tear.

My mother later referred to that day as "the happiest day of her life." My parents caused me to experience so many moments that have been difficult for me to share. I had never vocalized some of them, until now, and I have spent my life trying to forget them. Time has helped in my attempt to forget my childhood experiences, but the injustice remains forever etched in my memory.

"When you leave your family with no tears shed, it is not a family."

CHAPTER 23
New Beginnings

A few miles up the road, I pulled into the local post office. There was an elderly mail carrier who worked there, and I used to visit him a lot during my rides with Batch. He was always so kind, caring, and soft-spoken; a man I always wished I had as my dad. He thought I was a good girl and always praised my hard work. His eyes watered up when I told him I was leaving for good. "I don't blame you, Deb," he said. He reached into his pocket, pulled out a $20 bill to help me buy gas, but I could not take it. I asked to use his telephone, and called Cliff to let him know what had happened. He told me about his cousin who owned a large dairy cattle farm and told me to go there for the time being. I hugged my dear friend goodbye. He hugged me back tightly, his eyes conveying both sadness and a reassuring wink.

I headed north, on my way to Cliff's cousin's place, two hours from where I was. I spent more time watching my rearview mirror than my windshield, terrified that my father would try to chase me down. I kept seeing images of what would happen to me if my father caught up with me. I kept repeating to myself, "Everything is going to be okay." My legs were so weak I could barely press down on the accelerator. There were moments when my knee shook so uncontrollably that I had to grab it to hold it steady. I took many of the back winding roads to quickly disappear, and every mile that passed, I felt freedom becoming a reality. I was committed to the getaway, and nothing was going to turn me around.

When I made it to the farm where I would hide out for a few days, my mind and body were exhausted. I was still dreadfully fearful that my father would find me, but the farm was far out in the countryside and off a beaten path. I felt a little bit of comfort that he would not find me. The family was very welcoming, and that evening I helped them milk their dairy cows. When nighttime arrived, I asked if I could sleep in the barn, still fearful of being found by my father. For the next few nights, I slept on a couple of blankets on top of bales of hay, high up in the dark hayloft out of sight. I felt safe and comfortable amongst the animals; a place that had always been a safe haven for me.

On the third day, I was feeling more confident that my father would not find me, so I drove into the next town over to find a way to earn some money. I walked into an upscale restaurant and asked if there were any server positions open. They hired me on the spot! I was excited for the opportunity to support myself, and that evening I started my new job.

Cliff came to visit me at the farm and announced he had just given his notice at the horse farm and found us a little apartment nearby. His cousin offered to keep King at his farm, and Cliff applied for a job at the local lumber yard. I worked long hours as a server, taking on as many double shifts as possible. Cliff and I were settling in, securing our future together and I felt empowered by earning my own money.

A few weeks later, the owners of the restaurant came in to dine and requested me as their server. They brought their younger brother with them, who was very arrogant and kept making inappropriate comments to me while I was serving them. I was disgusted by his actions but kept a smile on my face. I was a new employee there and needed the job. Following their dinner, I cleared their table, and as I made my way to the kitchen through a dimly lit hall, the younger brother unexpectedly turned the corner and forcefully shoved me against the wall. He kept me pinned as he ran his hands across my chest. I was horrified and scared at the same time. I felt a burst of adrenaline and pushed him away, injuring my hand as I fought to escape his tight grip. After that, I no longer wanted to work there.

Not far from the restaurant was a computer company. I was surprised when I walked into the human resources department to see one of my old neighbors who used to buy firewood from me. My reputation of being a hard worker paid off. He hired me on the spot. I started on the factory floor, assembling computers all day long. It was not what I wanted to be doing, but I needed a solid job. I put my head down and worked hard. A few months later, Cliff and I were taking a drive back up to the dairy farm when he pointed to the glove compartment of the truck and said, "There is a ring in there for you." That was his way of proposing to me. I wished it could have been more romantic, but I knew his heart and I knew that was how he was. Months later, we set a wedding date. We had no extra money for an extravagant wedding, but it was still special. We were married in a little white country church and had our reception outdoors under the trees at the dairy farm. It was a perfect day.

After a year, we outgrew our tiny apartment and rented a house trailer that was older than both of us put together. It sat on a little pastureland that was calling my name to put some sheep on. I missed having sheep around me, but I simply could not afford to purchase any show sheep. I surrendered to the idea that it was going to be quite some time before I could purchase high-quality sheep. One day, my neighbor informed me of a large sheep farm nearby, and Cliff and I immediately made a drive to visit the place.

The farm was only about fifteen miles away, owned by an older gentleman who had raised sheep all his life. As we drove into his driveway, our eyes were treated to a classic stately New England farm, surrounded by old gray handmade stonewalls, many covered in green moss. There were beautiful white and pink fragrant apple and peach trees in peak blossom scattered around the property. Surely, they were planted years earlier to harvest their fruit for the working homestead. I made my way up the worn dirt path. A frail weathered man sporting an old faded pair of denim bib overalls with tattered rips greeted me kindly. An old frazzled straw hat rested almost sideways on his thin white hair. Proudly, he walked me around his homestead to show off his flock of sheep which consisted of close to three hundred. I was impressed at how well cared for they were. I could tell that their overall health was excellent. They were crossbred, mixed with two or more breeds; therefore, they could not be registered as show sheep. I instantly fell in love with them, and it warmed my heart to be standing amongst sheep in a pasture again. My heart felt like I belonged there. "They are sixty dollars each, if you want any," the man stated.

Show sheep typically range in price from five hundred to several thousand dollars each. I missed sheep immensely, and since they had a pasture to roam in, I could not say no. With pure elation, I said yes to purchase three. They were beautifully marked with their white faces and legs speckled with black splotches, as if an ink bottle had spilled randomly, splattering ink across them. Cliff helped me lift the sheep up one at a time into the back of our truck to bring them home. The entire ride, I sat sideways in my seat, never taking my eyes off them—I was so proud. The thought of showing nationally never left my heart, but at the time I felt like it would be an eternity before I could achieve that goal. They settled in perfectly and provided me comfort while filling a huge void in my soul.

CHAPTER 24

Hannah

After two years of living on our farm, I woke up one morning feeling quite ill. After a quick visit to the doctor's office, it was confirmed that I was expecting! We were both excited about the new addition coming to our family. A new chapter was about to begin in our lives. As the days progressed, I experienced extreme nausea that did not subside. I was losing so much weight my doctor admitted me to the hospital where I remained on an I.V. for several weeks.

One day, while my doctor was making his hospital rounds, he sat at my bedside and asked, "Don't you have a mother?" I briefly explained my situation, knowing he was kind and empathetic. He listened, then asked me for her telephone number. I was reluctant to give it to him, but I was so ill I foolishly thought she may care. Reaching over me, he lifted the room telephone off the hook and called my mother. The doctor explained who he was and why he was calling. He let her know I was incredibly ill and that he was calling because he thought she would want to know. My mother replied, "I don't care if she or the baby lives or dies." Then she simply hung up. I could see the disappointment on my doctor's face. He reached out to me, patted me on the shoulder and told me everything was going to be okay. "I will take good care of you," he promised. And that, he did.

For months, I was in and out of the hospital until Hannah was finally born. She was a perfectly healthy and happy full-term baby with blonde hair and blue eyes. It did not take long for Hannah to fall in love with those three sheep we had. Just as I had done, as soon as she learned to walk, she found her way to the barn to play with them. When she was four years old, Cliff and I purchased a purebred registered female sheep of her own, a Southdown, the same breed that my Porgy was. They are very mellow and smaller in size, making it an extremely popular breed for children. Hannah named her Flower and they immediately became best friends.

Hannah's very first show of her young life was at the largest youth show in New England. There were hundreds of competitors divided into various age groups. She and Flower were remarkably successful, bringing home the prize for winning the "Pixie" division for fitting and showmanship. Additionally, she brought home the grand trophy of an embroidered director's chair that read "Champion Pixie Showman."

Hannah was well on her way to a magnificent career that she genuinely loved and excelled at. Over the next ten years, she won the Champion Showman trophy in every single age division. When she was sixteen, she won the National Champion Showman award at the largest livestock show in the world, the North American International Livestock Exhibition in Louisville, Kentucky. Bill, a dear friend of hers, gave her a young calf to show along with her sheep the following summer. She added an interest in showing beef cattle. She was hooked for the rest of her life showing cattle and sheep. Hannah was highly respected by many for her natural God-given talents with both species.

At the annual Fryeburg fair, Hannah competed at the premier event for 4-H members in the baby beef show and sale. It is the one show that all the 4-H members in Maine and New Hampshire dream about winning. Each year after the competition, the names of the champion exhibitors are painted on a large board and nailed up on the overhead wall in the 4-H barn. It is a monumental goal for competitors to win their way up on the wall of fame. Hannah's last year in 4-H was in 1999. She culminated her 4-H career with her name on that wall four times. She made history as the only 4-H member in the 150 years of the competition to ever win both Grand Champion Lamb and Grand Champion Steer in the same year. Her photo was published in the fair history book that year for setting the record that still has not been broken.

Circles of spectators, newspaper reporters and photographers surrounded her, applauding and recording her special day. Cliff and I stood nearby overflowing with pride at her accomplishments, watching her receive both coveted awards. Cliff and I were watching the reporters interview her when suddenly I heard a loud, arrogant and familiar voice. I froze in fear. It was my father yelling from behind the crowd, "I taught her everything she knows." Cliff and I were flabbergasted at his audacity! From the day she was born, neither he nor my mother acknowledged her, yet he still tried to steal recognition for her accomplishments.

Hannah's sheep and cattle competitions were the catalyst for her thriving professional career. She was the one that breeders wanted to show their animals as her talents were so polished in the presentation of livestock. Many would comment, "Hannah could show a chicken and make it look like it deserved to be a national champion!" As soon as she graduated from high school, she was offered a job at one of the most elite Hereford and Black Angus Beef Cattle ranches in the country. LeGrand Ranch in Freeman, South Dakota invited her to join their elite show team, an enormous achievement for such a young person. Not long after settling into her new position, she telephoned home to tell Cliff and me she was showing cattle at the National Western Stock Show in Denver. "Mom and Dad, I am helping to fit a bull today that just won national champion Angus and sold for over $100,000!" The excitement in her voice was priceless. That bull won at the national competition with

Hannah's help. She enjoyed many years of professional fitting and showing cattle and sheep throughout the United States. A few years later, she met her future husband Juston when they both were showing cattle. My granddaughter, Emma Rae, is now following in our footsteps by showing cattle and show pigs. Three generations later, I guess one could say, "It was meant to be."

Deb's Reserve National Champion Ewe 1997

Handled by Hannah

CHAPTER 25

A King for a Farm

After a few years, we outgrew the old house trailer that was beyond repair because of its condition and age. The heating system and insulation were so poor that on winter mornings the walls inside were covered with white frost. It was miserable! We found a new property not too far away with even more pastureland. It even had a little old barn we could use to house the sheep. The home was a log cabin that we instantly fell in love with.

Mortgage interest rates were quite high in the 80s, so the rate for our loan was 14.5%. The bank agreed to write us a loan for the little farm with $1,500 down. That was an enormous amount for us but we both worked lots of extra hours to save enough for the down payment. On the day of our bank appointment, the idea of making payments for the next thirty years brought a mix of emotions including excitement, anxiety, and fear. When we hit the elevator button to the third floor of the bank, Cliff and I exchanged hugs. We reassured each other that we would somehow make it work. We settled down in front of the lender as he presented us with a bit of unexpected news. "We have a little problem," he said. "Instead of $1,500, we need $5,000 for the down payment." Our fluttering hearts crashed and my eyes filled with tears. It may as well have been $50,000 because we barely scraped up the $1,500. Cliff stood up and told the banker to keep the house, we could not afford it. He also delivered a few other choice words for not informing us until the moment we were to sign. We headed toward the exit door, when suddenly the banker flew up from his executive chair.

"Well, what do you have that is worth $5,000?" he asked.

"We own a Belgian stallion that is worth that much," Cliff answered.

"Do you have his registration paper?" the banker asked.

"We sure do."

The banker smiled.

"Well, we have never done this sort of thing before, but we will take your horse as collateral so you can purchase your farm today." Relieved, we sat back down, regained our composure and signed on all the dotted lines. Thanks to our beloved horse, King, we walked out of the bank that day with keys in hand to our new property! We quickly adjusted and were eager to embark on our next adventure. We formed lifelong friendships with our new neighbors, George and Pam.

Our dream to purchase more high-quality sheep was always on the forefront of our hearts. I subscribed to a monthly sheep magazine in order to stay informed about the industry. One morning, I was immersed in the pages of the magazine when Cliff approached and asked for a quick glimpse. Thumbing through the magazine, he noticed a full-page advertisement from an elite farm in New Hampshire with photos of their prize sheep. The caption read: "Show Sheep for Sale." Cliff looked over at me and said, "Why don't we take a ride and see them?" Of course, my answer was an enthusiastic yes! We immediately made plans to make the three-hour ride to check it out. We saw one of the most outstanding flocks of Dorsets I had seen in years!

We met with Jerry, the shepherd of the flock, who spent quality time showing us the entire operation. We viewed the glorious barns, fencing, and pastures filled with supreme quality sheep. I let him know we would love to purchase two females, but we did not have the budget to do so. I think Jerry could see my appreciation and enthusiasm for his sheep and wanted to help us out. He asked me which females I was interested in, and I pointed them out. "Well how about you just make payments to me and send me what you can along the way?" Jerry suggested. My heart was ready to explode with joy over his generous offer. We gave him a deposit and a handshake, promising to pay the balance soon. We happily loaded the two ewes onto the back of our truck. During the ride home, I did not take my adoring eyes off of them. Our new ewes were the ideal age to compete in the upcoming summer show. I felt a renewed sense of vitality. I was deeply grateful for Cliff enabling me to once again own top-quality show sheep. I named the best ewe "Miss Maine," who showed a lot of potential with her outstanding structure, and perfect breed type. We anxiously awaited the first opportunity we had to show our recent additions to the flock, and the time could not come fast enough. However, there was one monumental obstacle that I had to overcome. I would face my father for the first time in years at the competition.

CHAPTER 26

Face to Face with Fear

The thought of competing against my father scared me straight. But, my passion to compete with my new sheep was larger than my fear. I had come too far to allow fear of my father to weaken my dream. Besides, I had something to prove.

On the day we arrived for our first competition, we pulled in with our homemade plywood wooden trailer towed behind our old pick-up truck. We backed up to the barns to offload our two sheep, and one of the first voices I heard was my father's. He was bragging loudly to other exhibitors, showing off his expensive new aluminum sheep trailer. He pointed his finger in our direction, degrading our homemade rig. I held my head high, as I always did, and focused on the job at hand. Cliff and I were spending the next few days at the show, so I worked diligently at preparing my ewes for the competition. We did not own a camper trailer so we slept in sleeping bags on cots in the back of the sheep trailer. Back then, it was not unusual for exhibitors to make sleeping quarters in their trailers because the cost of camper trailers was too much for many.

When show day arrived, I pulled Miss Maine out of her pen to put the last-minute touches on her before entering the ring. My father and his "son" as he lovingly called him, purposely bumped into me. "You don't stand a chance," he sneered. To intimidate me, he made it a point to stand next to me in the lineup. When the judge instructed us to walk our sheep in a circle, my father pushed Miss Maine into the wall of the show arena with his knee, causing her to lose her balance. Others witnessed what he did, but no one said a word. I was not surprised that he pulled such a dirty stunt, but I was furious and concerned that Miss Maine may have been hurt. I kept my composure and quickly helped Miss Maine regain her balance. Throughout the class, my father and his so-called son made nasty remarks and snickered the entire time, making sure I heard them. However, it would take more than that to shake my confidence.

When the judge made his final decision, Miss Maine and I won second place in the class. My father won first place, and his mocking continued. The judge approached me and said, "Deb, your sheep look great today, you did a fine job." I was disappointed that I did not win first place, however, the judge fueled my enthusiasm with his encouragement. The purple champion rosette was awarded to my father, and he waved his ribbon in the air as if he had just won the lottery. As he was exiting the ring, he made it a point to brush his sheep against mine once again. After the show ended, we loaded our sheep in the back of our trailer and prepared to head to the next two shows. When we were ready to leave, my father backed his large new trailer right in front of ours. He parked so close, there was barely enough room between the two trailers to slide in a piece of paper. Even though he was trying to block us in, Cliff's skills from driving 18-wheeler trailer trucks enabled him to shimmy our rig around it. I knew my father was hoping we would scratch his new trailer, giving him a reason to come after us. As we drove away, my father yelled loudly over the crowd at us, "You live like a bunch of pigs in your trailer." I was humiliated to my core, but I kept my focus as we traveled to the next competition. We may have been traveling on a paper-thin budget, but my heart was still rich in hope and determination.

At the next competition, we unloaded our sheep and got them all settled in on fresh yellow straw for bedding and comfort. Arriving behind us were many trailers carrying prize livestock who were all vying for the win and prize money for the week. After a few hours, while I was busy tending to my sheep, another exhibitor, who I had profound respect for, approached me. He had been competing with his sheep professionally for over fifty years and was a man of few words. I was a bit surprised to see him standing in front of me. "Deb, I am disappointed in you," he said. My heart immediately sank, wondering why. "The Morris family just got sent home and their sheep are now quarantined for the rest of the summer. Someone reported that their sheep have a communicable disease. Your father just told me you were the one that reported them and got them kicked out. I didn't think you would do that to another breeder." I was appalled! The Morris family and their top-quality sheep were the ones to beat at the next few shows. My father knew it and had devised a plan to have them kicked out and blame it on me. He wanted to tarnish my name and make me look bad to the other breeders. His initiation of hateful gossip and attempt to darken my reputation was sickening, but not surprising. The truth eventually came out, but I knew my father was going to make it very rough for me to stay in the fight. I was just as determined to never give up.

Despite my father's effort to sabotage my reputation, Miss Maine won the Grand Champion and the Best in Show awards at that competition. We loaded up once again and headed to the next show, which was a week away. The judge at the next competition was a highly respected livestock judge from Maryland. The fair spared no expense in bringing him to Maine to judge the competition. Miss Maine was growing nicely, and I had her highly prepared and ready for presentation. As I had done so many times before, my ewe and I quietly and confidently entered the show ring to do our thing. I was aware of my father's previous behavior, so when he tried to edge me in the show ring, I pulled out of line and moved to another position away from him. Before the day had ended, Miss Maine had won both Grand Champion and the Best in

Show prize for two weeks in a row! The judges' comments about our presentation propelled my confidence. I set my eyes on entering the State Fair, the second largest and most competitive sheep show in New England. The State Fair competition was the same show that Porgy and I won the "Most Authentic" award in and took part in the parade. There was a tremendous amount of history on those grounds. It was where Cliff and I met and where Hannah made history, with her name displayed on the wall. Between Miss Maine's performance and the judges' encouragement, I was excited to go home and begin preparation for the state fair competition.

CHAPTER 27

Delayed, But Not Denied

For months, my excitement about the state competition grew. I submitted my entry well before the entry deadline. Because it was a week-long event, arrangements had to be made to handle farm chores and schedule time off from work. I checked the mailbox every day, anticipating our acceptance letter and entry passes to the show. I waited for days—no letter. With only days away from the show, we still had not received an acceptance letter. When I saw the mail carrier approaching our mailbox, I ran to meet him, not giving him time to put that anxiously awaited envelope in the box. Finally, the envelope from the fair arrived!! I was trembling with excitement as I opened it, but I could not believe my eyes. My entire body sank under the weight of immense disappointment when I pulled out the letter to see in dark capital letters, ENTRIES DENIED.

I could not believe my eyes! How could it be true? I had never been denied entry into a show in my life! The tears of disbelief and disappointment filled my day. All the months of anticipation and enthusiasm were gone, and it felt like a barrel of water had been thrown on my fire. We resolved to try again the following year. In the meantime, there was an upcoming sheep sale to be held in Ohio that spring offering some of the finest registered purebred sheep in the land. We had been saving money for the sale for months and hoped to bring home a top contender to add to our growing flock. For years, we have been wanting to attend that show, so we put our disappointment aside and with renewed excitement focused our attention to prepare for the trip to Ohio.

When we arrived at the sale in Ohio, there were several barns full of sheep available from all over the country to view prior to the auction. Each sheep was paint branded with a lot number on top of their backs. Breeders strolled around the barns examining the prospects while referring to the sale catalog which detailed their extended pedigrees. Cliff and I looked at all the fine candidates, hoping that we could bring one home with us. After much discussion and hours of looking, we decided "Lot 175" was the perfect specimen we wanted to bring back to Maine. As we were standing at her pen admiring her, I felt someone watching me. I glanced over my shoulder and spotted a familiar large dark shadow. My father was standing right behind me and with a large black marker I saw him write down LOT #175 on the clipboard he was carrying. I was shocked to see him there. He continued to follow Cliff and me around the barns. When we realized he was trying to intimidate us, we left the barns for a few hours.

At the auction the next morning, our hearts were set on Lot 175. Several hundred people were in attendance, and many sheep were selling for over $1,000 each. Cliff and I had barely scraped up $1,500 to spend on our pick, and we were praying it would be enough. Our favorite pick walked into the sale block, and she looked beautiful. I pictured myself showing her with pride. My heart was pounding with excitement as the auctioneer started his whaling of auctioning her off. Bids were coming in on her from every direction and the bid quickly reached $1,000. My arm was shaking so much, I could hardly hold it still to wave in another bid. The bids flowed from $1,000 to $1,200, to $1,300, to $1400. My heart stopped beating for a moment as I waved my trembling hand up in the air to $1500. My blood pressure felt so high I felt the pulse in my face.

"$1600!" I heard. I glanced behind me and saw my father holding up his hand.

The auctioneer shouted "$1600, do I have $1700? Any more bids?" The hammer dropped sharply on the desk. "SOLD." My father waved his bid number in the air with a grinch-like smirk as my mother sat beside him giggling. I was crushed. We made the fifteen-hour drive back home without a sheep, feeling emotionally drained from the heartbreak, disappointment, and disgust. I thought, *When will this ever end? Will they ever leave me alone and allow me to live my life without intimidation?*

Five years later, I submitted my entry again for the state show. Entries from the four previous years had all been denied but I was determined to keep trying. Weeks later, I strolled to the mailbox and saw a letter from the fair. Holding my breath, I tore open the envelope and the first thing I laid my eyes on were blue admission tickets and exhibitor passes! I unfolded the letter to more good news: CONGRATULATIONS! YOUR ENTRIES ARE ACCEPTED! I could barely contain my excitement. We were in!

We spent the next few weeks preparing for the three-hour drive to the state competition. When we finally arrived at the fairgrounds, we saw our names tagged on pens reserved just for us. We were greeted at check-in by the fair superintendent. We shared our enthusiasm about finally being accepted after years of being denied. The fair superintendent shared some shocking news with us.

"Well, I was warned by another exhibitor for the past five years to not accept your entries because you and your sheep weren't good enough to compete here," he admitted. I was speechless! I tried not to show any negative reaction when he mentioned my father's name as the one who passed along that information. At that point, I was just grateful to be accepted in the show and focus my energy on proving that my sheep and I were good enough.

The competitions ran for an entire week, with various species and breeds scheduled to compete for the fair's coveted honors. There was considerable prize money attached to the prestigious "Grand Herdsman Award." It would be awarded to the one exhibitor deemed to be the most outstanding caretaker over all the species of livestock on the fairgrounds. The winners were determined by a point system consisting of several elements. Sportsmanship, cooperation, care and presentation of livestock, stall attractiveness, along with educational material displayed for the public to learn about livestock were the categories which were considered. After five years of waiting, we won the State Grand Champion Female and advanced on to win the "Best in Show" award after competing against over four hundred other sheep. On the last day of the fair, the arena was packed with hundreds of exhibitors standing arm to arm intently waiting for the fair president to make the announcements. We quietly listened as they awarded the Herdsman Award to a wonderful large dairy farm family that had been attending the show for over thirty years. We were ecstatic when we heard the announcer say, "This year, the Shepherd's Award is going to Cliff and Debby Jo Holmquist." We joyfully received the beautiful marble trophy, which was an absolute treasure! The president then looked down at his notepad and began calling off the winners of the Grand Herdsman Award. He called the names of the third-place winner, then the second-place winner before making a special announcement. "The winner of this year's Grand Herdsman Award, for the first time in the history of this fair, is going to a sheep breeder for their magnificent presentation. The winners are Cliff and Debby Jo Holmquist!" The crowd erupted and all I can remember is other exhibitors grabbing my arm and saying, "You won, you won!" It felt like a blur, all happening in slow motion. I could not believe our names were just called to win that magnificent honor. I glanced over my shoulder and saw my father standing at the rear of the crowd in silence.

That evening, as we were loading our prize sheep into our trailer to return home, the livestock superintendent approached me with an outstretched hand and squeezed my hand so hard it hurt. He patted me on my back and said, "Deb, I am sorry you were misjudged for so long. I sincerely apologize for that. I hope you return next year to be with us." I gave him my utmost thanks and replied, "We certainly will!" And that we did, year after year for many years.

For the next sixteen years in a row, we won first place flock, the Grand Champions award, and Best in Show. Over the years, we invested every ounce of dedication, determination and funds to increase our little flock. In 1989, we had fifteen sheep which were performing very well and earning many top titles around New England.

CHAPTER 28

Mountain Mainiac

The Ohio Dorset Show and Sale was one of the most prestigious events in the industry. We submitted entries for one ewe and one ram lamb who we affectionately named "Mainiac." We thought it was a clever and appropriate name for him since we were from Maine. Mainiac exhibited great structure and breed type, along with a world of promise in his future. Our female ewe, "Pine Cone" was a pretty sheep and particularly good in her own right. It was our first time selling our bloodline and competing against hundreds of the best in the nation from coast to coast. We were excited to be going up against the "big boys." We proudly hung our little homemade green and white farm sign above them that read "West View Farm," along with their pedigree cards so potential buyers could view their extended pedigrees. They were white as snow and trimmed smooth as velvet to catch the judges' eye. As I glanced around the three barns, I was surrounded by some of the highest quality sheep I had ever seen in one place. Sheep from large California farms that had been exhibiting for many years were there, along with entries from the midwestern states of Iowa, Illinois, Ohio, and Indiana. I wondered how a little farm from Maine would fare as the new kids on the block.

On show day, I walked Mainiac into the show ring, which was laden with green carpet, proudly holding his head high. There were at least fifty other rams lined up for his class. The judge moved through the line, carefully handling and examining each one. He felt their muscling, length of body, evaluated their breed type and overall correctness. He instructed our class to walk once around in a large circle, then line up head to tail so that he could take one last glance at their side view. As the judge observed the lineup, comparing one to another, he pointed his finger to the class selection that was at the bottom of his list. They were pulled out of the lineup. After pulling out the bottom forty-five, his top five selections were still standing head to tail, including my Mainiac. I could feel my pulse pounding in my forehead from the pressure as the judge selected his bottom four to eliminate. He pointed his finger to the ram behind me, and then there were four. He pointed again—three, then two. Last, he pointed his finger at me and said, "First." My legs felt like cooked spaghetti, and I had to remind myself to breathe. Mainiac had just won first place!

Several breeders came in the ring to handle the first five placings, and get a sneak peek before they sold. We received several compliments. Mainiac was resting comfortably nibbling on small handfuls of luscious green alfalfa hay to keep him content until he was called back for the finals about forty-five minutes later. He picked the perfect day to behave nicely as we made our way to the ring. After a few minutes of watching the judge go through his paces, he turned to the judge's table and reached for his microphone. It was standing room only as the judge complimented the body structure and excellent breed type of each of the competitors. He congratulated each exhibitor for breeding such fine specimens, and then we braced ourselves for the final decision. "I will now shake hands with today's Junior Champion," he announced. He approached me and Mainiac, extended his hand to me, tipped his hat, and said, "Congratulations ma'am." The sales manager placed the beautiful bright purple champion rosette around Mainiac's neck and stamped a large purple paint brand in the form of a rosette on top of his back. It was a day I had dreamed of for over twenty-five years. Our hard work and dedication were becoming more evident.

The next day, all the sheep shown on the previous day were ready to appear for the auction. Mainiac walked proudly into the sale block while the auctioneer read his pedigree aloud and bragged to the audience. "Here is a stud ram that came all the way from Maine." The bids flew in fast and furious, and the hammer slammed down. "SOLD" at $2,750!" Most of the sheep that day sold for about $700, so that was a remarkable price! Mainiac was purchased by a top-seasoned breeder from Illinois who planned to show him that summer and use him for breeding. Our ewe lamb, Pine Cone, stood fourth out of over fifty in her class, also selling well to a wonderful farm in Iowa.

On our 15-hour drive home, it felt like we were riding on a flying carpet propelled by the high winds of pure elation. We reminisced about our past few days for the entire ride. Upon returning home, our neighbors taped congratulatory posters with party streamers all around our sheep barn and on the front door of our house. They wanted to show how proud they were of us for how we represented the state of Maine. It touched our hearts deeply. Subsequently, Mainiac was shown by his new owner that entire summer and won Grand Champion Ram at every single competition. He was also a member of the Champion Dorset Flock at the largest sheep show in the world. The breeder who purchased him wanted other breeders to think he was the one who raised Mainiac. He cut out the ear tag that had our farm name imprinted on it and replaced it with a tag bearing his name. It wasn't the first time someone had tried to take credit for all of my hard work.

While competing at a local show with my sheep, a friend approached me and asked if I had any sheep for sale. I had three, so he told me he would pass my number on to his friend. He owned a large farm and wanted to put some sheep on it. Shortly thereafter, I received a call from his friend, Connor, who had heard we had a wonderful reputation and high-quality sheep. After a brief conversation, he reserved three sheep to purchase. The following weekend, Cliff and I loaded up three beautiful sheep and headed to his farm. When he said he lived up in the mountains, he was not kidding! We turned off of the main road to take his road, which was a very steep uphill drive. We kept going higher and higher. Finally, our eyes were met with a glorious spread of immaculate rolling pastures surrounded by miles of old weathered gray stone walls. These old walls were used to keep the sheep in before wire fencing was manufactured. Ironically, the farm was one of the largest sheep farms in the area over 150 years ago! The farm had a few hundred immaculately maintained rolling acres with breathtaking views at every angle of the mountain range capped by snow.

We were greeted by Connor and his wife Shelly as we backed our trailer up to offload their new purchases into a stately red barn. They were thrilled with the look of their new sheep and excited to have them roaming their beautiful pastures. They were also excited that one sheep was pregnant and due to have her baby lambs in a few weeks. We left them with detailed instructions on how to maintain the lambs and gave them an invitation to call us, day or night, if needed. After a few weeks, one ewe had twins. Connor called to ask for our help because he had never been exposed to anything like that. Cliff and I were happy to make the drive up and spend time with them to educate and show them how to care for the recent additions to their livestock. It was a whole new world for them. Connor was quite intrigued and grateful for the knowledge we shared. We drove back down the mountainside, riding the brakes the entire time, hoping we would not slide off. We were envious of the sheep having such a gorgeous home, yet satisfied that they would have a wonderful life.

After the summer had passed, Cliff and I continued working full-time jobs while slowly building our flock of sheep. We had just finished building a small, beautiful sheep barn that was surrounded by a solid corral. The corral had several pens inside to comfortably house the show sheep. Additionally, there was an office in one corner to conduct sheep sales and handle all the corresponding paperwork. We also built a second-floor hayloft to hold a few hundred bales of hay for winter feed. One evening, we received an unexpected call from Connor that changed the trajectory of our lives in a moment.

Cliff Assisting a Newborn Lamb

CHAPTER 29

An Offer of a Lifetime

"Hello, Deb. This is Connor," he began. "You know, I have been thinking about your sheep project. I have the money and the land, and you have the knowledge and experience. How about we form a partnership and raise some of the best sheep in the country?" I am positive my heart stopped beating momentarily when I heard his offer. We scheduled a date for him to stop by our farm the following week to discuss the details of our partnership. I hung up the telephone and could not wait to share the news with Cliff. Later, Connor stopped by to discuss our new venture. He lived near the Sugarloaf Ski Resort, so we called our new flock "Sugarloaf Dorsets." Connor passed me a checkbook with a substantial balance in it and told me to use what we needed to get started. I was humbled and honored.

"Well, I heard you are a hard worker. You know what you are doing, and you know where you want to go," he said. My heart melted like a stick of butter in a hot cast iron pan. I barely knew him, yet he was extending a tremendous amount of faith and trust in me. Within the next two weeks, Cliff and I gave our two-week notices and put our little farm up for sale. The farm sold quickly. We took our sheep and what equipment we owned and headed to the mountains to experience a monumental life change.

Connor owned a condominium at the ski resort twenty miles from the farm, and that became our new home. We were not used to living in such a delightful place with a bird's-eye view of the ski trails! It was magnificent, but extremely cold. During our first week at the new farm, Connor asked my opinion about purchasing more sheep. I told him about a farm in Ohio that had a stellar reputation that I had admired for years. I knew the owner and had a lot of trust in him. "Why don't you fly out there and pick out the best six you can find?" Connor suggested. A few days later, he secured plane tickets for Cliff and me to meet with the owner to make our selection of the sheep we wanted to purchase.

On a bitterly frigid January day, we were greeted with wonderful hospitality as we entered the old homestead of Jarrod and Luna. The smell of homemade biscuits and spicy hot chili simmering in a cast-iron pot on their woodstove filled the air. Over a delectable dinner, we discussed the pedigrees of his sheep extensively. The entire time, I could barely sit still, eager to go to the barn to see all the sheep. When Jarrod said we would go to the barn to look them over first thing in the morning, I could not contain my excitement.

"Could we go look at them now?" I asked.

He chuckled and said, 'Let's Go"!

We put on warm winter outwear and pushed through the freezing winds to the barn.

We were immensely impressed with the over three hundred sheep standing in front of us. They were separated into age groups in various pens and everything was clean and well organized. In one pen, there was a group of 150 lambs that had been recently weaned from their mothers. Jarrod stood back and quietly observed us for a few moments. I thought he did it to watch what our reaction to the group would be and how I would approach our selections. With confidence, I asked him for some gates so we could gather them up into groups carefully without startling them. He had several handy, so we pulled a few in and quietly set up a large catch pen to hold all 150. It did not take me long to cut out several that I did not take a shine to. Jarrod tended the gate for me as I released five at a time until I got down to about the top twenty.　　Jarrod was surprised at how quickly I made my decision. Once I had my top twenty, I spent more time analyzing them to get my picks down to my top six. After selecting my top six, Jarrod shook his head and said, "This would never happen again, but these were my favorite six as well." He proved it by showing me his record book with the exact six he had chosen as his show ewes for the coming year. Each displayed a red star by their ear tag number on his chart, confirming he was not just telling me what I wanted to hear to appease me. I wrote their numbers down on the notepad in my jacket for safekeeping. He knew then that he had a qualified buyer. No prices were discussed until we returned to the house for hot tea. When we stepped back into the warm kitchen, Jarrod's Uncle Carl was sitting at the dinner table. He was a jolly soul, in his late seventies, whose stature was rounder than he was tall. As he spoke, he looked over his eyeglasses, not through them. As a well-known attorney in town who oversaw the finances of Jarrod's farm, he was the negotiator of the family. Jarrod informed him of my selections as Uncle Carl smiled when he learned we had both chosen the same six.

The time came for me to ask their price. Jarrod turned to Uncle Carl as he was quickly scratching figures on a piece of paper. Uncle Carl said, "You know it isn't every day someone can just come in and pick out the best six. This is not going to be cheap." He wrote the figure down and slid it across the table to me. It was close to what I expected it to be, and I understood that it was a unique opportunity to come in and hand-pick the best out of 150. I was confident with my choices, pulled out my checkbook and wrote the check. We finalized the plan for their transport to Maine, traded firm handshakes and celebrated my special purchase. It was an important sale for their farm and a critical piece to add to our foundation.

It did not take long for word to get out around the sheep circles that there was a new partnership forming with some good sheep. I received a telephone call one day from Dale, one of the nation's top breeders in the Midwest. Dale heard we were in the market for top sheep to add to our flock and informed me that his flock of 175 may be for sale. He had been in business for many years successfully, winning national champion titles and selling record high sheep. I had an enormous amount of respect for him and his flock. Dale invited us to travel to his farm, which was also in Ohio, to view his flock and see what we thought. We made the drive to his farm in the early spring and were warmly greeted by Dale and his wife Stella. They rolled out the red carpet for us with a wonderful home-cooked meal of prime rib with red wine and all the fixings. After dinner, Dale presented me with a notebook filled with hundreds of entries with extended pedigrees on each sheep he currently had in his flock. It was an impressive sight to view the enormous details on each bloodline for multiple generations he had sketched out. Dale had a master's degree in genetics, and it showed. We were immensely impressed. Just like Jarrod's farm, it was exceptionally clean and well-organized, just what one might expect from a professional farm. The sheep were penned in large groups by age, so it was convenient to look them all over. We spent the next few hours examining them and learning much about them. Cliff and I left the farm for the evening, extremely excited about the opportunity. I quickly called Connor to give him our opinion of what we had seen. He simply replied, "Buy them for what you think they are worth." Cliff and I then sketched out the quantities in each age group and what we thought was an appropriate purchase price. I wrote that six-figure amount down on a small piece of paper and placed it in my jacket pocket for safekeeping.

Early the following morning we strolled back to the barn, taking one more look at the marvelous specimens. I told Dale we were interested in purchasing the entire flock and promised to continue their genetic excellence going forward. "What is your price for the 175 head?" I asked. His answer was the exact dollar amount I had written. I smiled as I passed my piece of paper to him. I am sure the odds of that were very slim. We exchanged firm handshakes and congratulations to one another. Together, we made plans to transport our new purchase 1,400 miles back to Maine. As Cliff and I were readying to leave, a young black kitten was sitting on the fencepost by the barn. Dale said, "The sheep don't leave here without the kitten." We scooped her up and laid her in the back seat of the truck on a blanket where she slept all the way home. "Louie" became a beloved family member for the next seventeen glorious years. We joked for many years about the six-figure kitten we had to buy to get the sheep!

A month later, we arranged for a double-decked 18-wheeler livestock trailer to pick the flock up for their long ride to their new home. Twenty hours later, the big rig backed up to our barn in Maine. Each sheep carefully made their way down the ramp, stepping foot on Maine ground. Every single one made the trip perfectly. Our elite flock had grown close to 250 head of sheep and were scattered in various barns on the farm. During one of Connor's visits to the farm, he noticed.

"We need a bigger barn, don't we?" Connor asked.

"Yes, we do" I replied.

Connor was best friends with a local builder in town, so a meeting was scheduled immediately to sketch out a new barn. We spent a good part of the day planning out what we needed. The plan included barn dimensions of 150 feet long by sixty feet wide. The barn would have a heated nursery room, washroom in which to wash the show sheep, office and a grain room. Outside the grain room, six-ton grain bins would auger the grain inside the barn. Cliff and I designed grain feeders that ran the length of the barn on both sides of a cement middle aisle. It enabled us to feed quickly and efficiently with the ability to keep it swept clean. We had custom-made solid steel gates outside for exercise yards for each pen, and the length of the barn on both sides. A large second-floor hayloft was constructed to hold several thousand bales of hay for winter feed. During the process, Connor noted we were still living twenty miles away from the farm, which made it difficult to be near the sheep during lambing time. He told the builder to include living space on the third floor for Cliff, Hannah, and myself. That would place us within twenty steps down the staircase to tend the sheep. We were thrilled!

The contractor put a large crew on the project and in three months' time, our beautiful barn was completed. We installed a beautiful custom-made bronze sheep weathervane on top of the large cupola in the middle of the roof. It was a majestic red barn painted with white trim that was officially a sheep barn and our home. Our barn became a model sheep barn for new sheep farmers in Canada. The Governor of Maine visited our flock frequently, and so did the Department of Agriculture of Canada. Busloads of tourists pulled into our driveway on many occasions, to take photos, ask questions, and take notes. A television show was filmed in our barn regarding our life of breeding and showing sheep. It was also featured on the front covers of many magazines.

The summer months passed quickly as we settled into our new lives on the mountaintop farm. We set our sights to attend the national show in Louisville, Kentucky. It was the largest livestock show in the world, boasting over 30,000 head of livestock with 5,000 sheep included. That was my dream! I wanted the partnership with Connor to be successful, since he had placed so much trust and faith in my abilities.

The national show was the equivalent of a livestock Olympics, and I entered our best four sheep. We had worked diligently with them for months, preparing them for the competition. They had to be in the exact body condition required for show sheep, so the feeding aspect of these sheep was critical. They could not be too fat or too lean; that's why it's called Animal Science. It truly is a science to learn and apply the critical feeding, managing, fitting, and showing skills to be successful. The sheep also had to pass a veterinarian health inspection before travel and carry health papers for admission to the show. When the time came for us to load up our trailer for the week-long competition, we checked everything off our list. We were confident we had remembered everything. As we shut the trailer door, we heard a "meow." Startled, we looked inside and there was Louie, the black kitten we brought home from Ohio, comfortably sitting in with the sheep! She must have thought she was supposed to go with them. I took her back into the barn, leaving her with a kiss before we left. We lived less than an hour's drive from the Canadian border, so we were facing a long journey. We drove twenty-six hours straight through to Kentucky. Our truck pulled in at the show arena in the wee hours of the morning, seeing nothing but neon lights all around us. I felt like we were driving up to the castle of the Wizard of Oz, it appeared so magical.

The sheep slept while riding. They had nourishing feed and water in their pens so when we offloaded them from the trailer, they were ready to settle in for the next several days. The sheep were stalled in the south wing of the convention center. It was filled from corner to corner with sheep as far as you could see. Farms from every area of the nation were represented. It was a remarkable sight to be amongst the grandeur of livestock. We proudly hung our "Sugarloaf Dorsets of Maine" sign over our pens and decorated them with green and white handmade banners with white lights on top. We also brought four small Maine balsam trees with us to use as decorations at the ends of our stalls. People noticed our sign as they walked by and commented on how far we had traveled to be at the show. Connor had made plans to fly in to attend. This would be his first time witnessing a show of such caliber.

"Emerald" was among the four sheep I picked out to make the trip. She was a gem in my eyes. She was one of the lambs I chose nine months earlier out of that group of 150 lambs in Ohio. At that time, she showed great promise, this would be her test. We sported a professional look, wearing crisp new white pressed show shirts with our farm name and logo embroidered in turquoise and purple on the back. Thirty minutes before the show began, I excused myself so I could have a few moments alone. I walked out of the barn and around the corner. Here, I found a quiet spot to kneel and say a quick prayer. When I returned to the sheep pens, my heart was already beating out of my chest in anticipation and nervousness. I was about to walk into the largest livestock show on earth. The class was so large, multiple circles had been formed around the ring to fit all the entrants in.

That day, God answered my prayers. After five hours of non-stop competing, we won the National Champion Ewe title with Emerald, and Reserve National Champion Ram with the one ram we brought along. Connor was overjoyed at our results and mesmerized by the high level of competition. He congratulated us on a job well done and expressed how proud he was of us. Connor smiled warmly as Cliff and I posed while photographers from the national sheep magazine snapped photos of us holding our champions. "I have an idea this is just the beginning for you guys" the photographer said.

As parting gifts to friends we had made, we gave away our four Maine balsam trees. We returned home with a Gold and Silver Award at our first-ever national competition. Tears of joy spilled from my eyes for our achievement. I was overwhelmed with a sense of belonging in the sheep career I had longed for my entire life. That day, I knew dreams really do come true if you never give up.

For the following ten years, we returned to the national championships and earned more top awards, with many of our sheep garnering "highest selling sheep" accolades. None of this came easily. I have always prided myself on being a hard worker. I have to say, these years were the absolute hardest I had ever worked in my life. It had been demanding, physically, emotionally, and mentally, but we were married to our project. We knew it required dedication, second to none. There was intense pressure involved in earning our way to the top, and even more to stay there.

The Sheep Barn in The Mountains - 1991

CHAPTER 30
Broke Back in the Mountains

We were honored to host many tour groups, school outings, livestock judging teams, 4-H meetings, and various educational seminars for agricultural departments. During one of those educational seminars, there was a large crowd in attendance at the barn. I had to walk up to the office to pick up some paperwork for a student. As I walked by our grain room, I heard people in there talking. The sliding door to the grain room was usually shut, so in my curiosity, I opened the door. There were two people sneaking handfuls of our custom-made grain out of the wheelbarrow and putting the grain into plastic baggies. They slipped the baggies into their coat pockets.

One of those individuals was a professor at an Ivy League college. I was shocked and disgusted to witness their behavior, especially from someone of that caliber. I politely but sternly requested they empty their samples back into the wheelbarrow and demanded they shut the door as they found it. Our grain was custom mixed in Quebec and we never intended to share our private mixture with anyone. We worked for years by trial and error to design our special blend of grain. What a shock to see people stooping so low to steal samples to have them analyzed.

During the fall and spring seasons, several hundred baby lambs are born, requiring all hands-on deck, 24/7. The winters are brutally cold in the mountains of Maine, with enormous amounts of snow. We spent many all-nighters during lambing time to ensure every lamb would survive. Our heated nursery room was an integral part of helping them survive the brutal winters. We kept the heat at 35 degrees. Once the mothers and babies graduated back out with the older lambs, the temperature change was not too extreme for them. The nursery was designed with white washable walls and a concrete floor with water drains in the middle. It held fifteen individual pens for new mothers who stayed in this room for five days. After the five days, they graduated back out into the population. After each group, we would tear down all the individual pens. All bedding was cleaned. The walls and floor were scrubbed with hot soap and water. We then reset it all up for the next round with clean fresh bedding in each pen. We performed that routine hundreds of times, which required hours of physical work. When it snowed, there were feet of snow that fell. Cliff spent days plowing around the farm to keep our roadways open. He also kept our outside corrals plowed so the older sheep could go outside for exercise.

We grew and mowed our own hay. It was baled in the summer and fall. Thousands of bales had to be picked up in the field by hand. They were stacked on trucks and trailers, then hauled up the steep hill, for about a mile, to the farm. The bales were unloaded one at a time, and stacked in the hayloft in sweltering heat. This was all to ensure we had a sufficient amount of hay during the winter months. There was never an idle moment year-round. We were happy spending our lives together, doing what we loved and enjoyed most. I would not have traded that life for anything in the world.

One frosty fall night, I had just returned from the airport about 100 miles away. I had put Hannah on a plane headed to Louisville for the nationals. Cliff had left days earlier, driving the sheep there. It was after 9:00 p.m. and I was late starting the feeding. I was alone in the barn, so chores took me an extra-long time that night. There was a tall aluminum ladder in place that I used to climb twenty feet up to reach the loft. I climbed up, threw down twenty-five bales, and walked over to make my return trip down. I turned around, stepped one foot on the top rung, then the second foot, putting all my weight on the top rung. Suddenly, the ladder slipped out from underneath me, and I felt myself falling. The next thing I remember was lying on the cold concrete floor on my back unable to move for what seemed like minutes. I was frightened out of my mind and felt excruciating pain searing through my entire body. I struggled to breathe. Based on the horrendous pain, I was convinced I had broken my back. I was petrified that I might have been paralyzed. *No, I will not just lay here,* I thought as I somehow forced myself to roll over. My two beloved cocker spaniels knew something bad had happened and were licking my face trying to comfort me. I was so grateful they were with me, as I felt so alone knowing there was no one around. I had to figure out a way to get help.

We had a barn telephone hanging on a post about thirty feet away. The piercing pain in my right arm convinced me it must be broken badly. I could not use it. I crawled inches at a time on my left arm across the cold concrete floor to the telephone. The phone was hanging about four feet up in the air on a barn beam. Somehow, I knocked the cord to pull it off the receiver. I called 911 and was relieved to hear a voice. The closest hospital ambulance was thirty miles away, so it would take some time for them to arrive. I continued to lie on the cold floor until help arrived with my two dogs never leaving my side. I spent the night in the trauma center receiving care. My right arm was broken in three places. One vertebra in my back was broken, and I suffered deep muscle tears across my buttocks. That particular injury came from landing on the fallen ladder. My entire body was black from bruising, and excruciating pain raced through me like I had never felt in my life. I was scheduled to fly to Kentucky in two days. It was the nationals—I had to be there. I had always heard that the pain after an accident was worse, and I found that statement to be true.

There was no way I would make my trip to Kentucky. I was heartbroken. The pain from missing that event hurt way more than my physical pain. The best I could do was wait at home until Cliff telephoned me with the results. In the group I sent was a ram I had raised named "Dream Maker." I was excited to show him there because I knew he stood a good chance of placing high. Sure enough, Cliff called to tell me he had won the National Champion Ram title. Tears flowed down my face from happiness and from the sadness that I was not there to be a part of it. I recovered quickly from my injuries and was determined to get back in with the sheep. Just a few days later I was carrying a feed bucket with one arm. My back, however, has continued to haunt me.

CHAPTER 31
Broken and Empty Promises

For over ten years we enjoyed living a magnificent life doing exactly what we wanted to be doing. We had just returned from Kentucky after winning our 15th national championship. Cliff and I were also honored to be awarded third place in the prestigious "Shepherds Award" amongst hundreds of exhibitors. A few days later, Connor telephoned me requesting a short meeting in the barn office. Cliff and I were expecting a celebratory meeting to congratulate us on our amazing wins. Connor, always a man of few words, stoically walked into the office and simply stated "I just sold the farm and we have 30 days to disperse the sheep." My body went into instant shock.

A numbness came over me and my brain went blank. It was as if someone had just shot me dead. My entire body became like a wet dishrag, and a pain set in my chest. I sat there for a few moments, feeling ill, unable to speak. I got up from my chair and quickly stepped out of the office, out the back door of the barn, and vomited repeatedly. I sobbed so hard I lost my breath. We had clawed our way to become one of the most respected and accomplished breeders in the nation, making history time after time. Our sheep were selling extremely high while earning a solid income. We had achieved what many had not. I thought to myself, *How can this be happening?* In that moment, I felt my soul dying like a wilted flower. I did not want to leave Cliff in the office too long absorbing the horrible news alone. I forced my way back, still not able to speak. Connor quietly rose to his feet and said, "You will need to find a buyer for all the sheep," then walked out and shut the office door. I sensed no emotion as we watched him drive away down the hill.

It was a devastating blow that completely shattered my life. We were in a difficult situation with no job, income, or home, and the added responsibility of finding a place for 250 sheep. Our lives were shattered. The thought of breaking up our nationally known flock of sheep that we had meticulously built over the past ten years was something we could not wrap our heads around. There were so many questions. How could I keep the flock together and keep it going? Would there be a way? I needed to find an answer in less than thirty days. I thought back to some of my best customers who were also good friends, who might have an interest. I called a close friend of ours, Rick, who had previously purchased two of our national champions. I knew it would be difficult to find someone who could purchase our flock for what they were worth.

Rick was incredibly sympathetic and said he was honored we asked him to purchase the flock. I gave him the price and provided him with Connors' name and telephone number so they could negotiate and handle the financial aspect of the deal between themselves. I confirmed their conversation had taken place, and Connor advised he had received a solid deposit. All was a go. Rick immediately offered to become partners with us just as Connor had been. We would continue managing the flock as if nothing had changed. We were so grateful when Rick volunteered to pay us a good salary starting immediately. He tossed around the idea of us moving to Ohio with the sheep, but agreed that it was best for them to stay in Maine. Cliff and I felt air flowing through our lungs again, with a feeling of hope that all would be okay. We were certainly going to miss our mountaintop home and farm, but we were thankful that our flock could remain together. However, we still faced an enormous task and adjustment ahead of us.

A close friend of ours heard about our situation. He knew of a thirty-acre farm that had just come up for sale within ten miles of where we had originally lived. We immediately drove to meet with him and investigate the property. It was perfect for us. There was a cute modest home on the land and barn that was even larger than our mountain-top barn. The next morning, we contacted the realty company to arrange the purchase of our new farm.

The exasperating job of packing our personal belongings, sheep equipment, supplies, and the sheep themselves took weeks. Our new farm was over one hundred miles away. We had made twenty-one trips with a truck and trailer to move everything. It was a grueling and heartbreaking undertaking to prepare to leave the home we had shared for the past eleven years. We saved the loading of the sheep for last, and it was extremely challenging. As we backed up three larger trailers to the barn, they knew something was about to happen and they did not like it. They were content at the home where they had always been. Many of them had been born there, and their reactions to the impending move made me sad. After getting them all loaded, I shut the last trailer door. We headed down the road toward our new home with heavy hearts and tears flowing. We learned that life has no guarantees, and promises are not always kept.

It took a lot to settle into our new environment, but we made it work. We kept a cheerful outlook and tried to keep things as normal as possible, looking at it as a bump in the road. On the day Rick drove to Maine to take care of the banking paperwork, we enjoyed a nice lunch together. Then, we all hopped into his truck to drive into town. We met with the bank representative who asked Rick if he was going to make a deposit. "Oh, I forgot my checkbook. I will mail it to you next week," Rick replied. He had always paid for sheep he purchased from us, some for several thousand dollars. He had always paid on time, so, I trusted him. After we left the bank, Rick said that we needed to have new business cards and stationery printed with his name on them as the new partner. We found a local print shop and placed our order, paying extra to have them printed in color. Upon returning to the farm, Rick meticulously inspected all the sheep. We continued discussing our plans and he assured us of his unwavering commitment. After spending the night with us, he left before dawn the next morning and promised to stay connected.

The next week I had not heard from Rick, so I called the bank to see if his deposit had arrived. It had not. Two weeks turned into three weeks, then four weeks. With no communication from Rick and still no deposit, Cliff and I were concerned. Weeks earlier, we had ordered a large load of grain that cost over $2,000. We were continuing to absorb other costs for the sheep. Something had to give, quickly! My instinct told me to get a job locally so we would have some funds to live on. I was hired immediately at the local veterinary clinic, which was a short drive away.

After waiting three months, we finally heard from Rick. He promised to send "that deposit" to the bank immediately along with extra funds to catch up on expenses we had incurred. The grain bill along with the purchase of hay, bedding, utilities, and needed supplies was accumulating to an uncomfortable level. I was the only one employed, so I applied for a short-term loan to cover the over $10,000 in expenses we had incurred. Cliff returned to the company he had left and went back to driving 18-wheelers. They were happy to have him back. After eight months of unanswered telephone calls to Rick, we still had not received the salary, reimbursement, or the deposit he had promised.

Our hearts were in the gully. We were still incurring costs with no reimbursement in sight. Additionally, we had the burden of caring for a large number of sheep. Our national show was only three weeks away and I was feeling distraught and disappointed by Rick's empty promises. We could not incur any more debt. Out of desperation, I did some background searching to find a way to contact Rick's wife. I had never met her and did not even know her first name. With the help of a mutual friend, I secured a telephone number for her. I prepared for an uncomfortable but necessary conversation. I prayed she would not hang up on me as I dialed her number. With a deep breath and a tremble in my voice, I introduced myself to Rick's wife, Lana. I gave her a brief overview of who I was, and told her of our arrangement with Rick. After explaining our situation to her, I felt my chest deflate. She exclaimed, "Oh my God! Tell me this is not true!"

Lana became emotional and her voice broke. I could hear her crying as she apologized profusely. She informed me that Rick had filed for bankruptcy, and they had just finalized their divorce. Emphatically she said, "I promise I will make Rick make this right for you." She requested that I document everything he had promised and all that had transpired since his commitment to us. She gave me a fax number to fax the information to her. There was an urgency with her request because she wanted to present it to her attorney as soon as possible. When I hung up the telephone, I laid my head down on my desk and sobbed.

With the nationals only two short weeks away, I was crushed at the thought that my strong flock of sheep could not compete because we simply could not afford to go. I regained my composure and pushed forward to type up Rick's promises, along with all of the expenses we had incurred since our agreement with him. It took hours to complete the documentation. I did not leave my computer until it was finished and faxed over to Lana. I telephoned Jarrod, a long-time attorney friend of mine, to let him know all that had transpired with Rick. He was not very optimistic that we could recover our losses since Rick had filed for bankruptcy. We brainstormed our options. I asked Jarrod how we might fare if we asked Rick to sign over the entire flock to us. His response did not bring comfort. "That will never happen," he said. A few days later I received a call from Lana.

Lana had given my notes to her attorney who requested a meeting with me, Cliff, and our attorney. She indicated that she had demanded that Rick be at the meeting as well. I expressed my greatest gratitude for her help and immediately contacted Jarrod. He agreed to make himself available for the conference call and promised to do whatever he could to help. That Friday, Cliff and I drove into town to Jarrod's office to prepare for the conference call. Jarrod was apprehensive and suggested that we may not recover the $30,000 in expenses we had incurred or the salary we had been promised. We all sat around the table as Jarrod dialed the number to Lana's attorney. My body was weak with fear of what the outcome would be. Lana's attorney answered on the second ring. With a friendly tone he informed us that Lana and Rick were sitting beside him. I expected Rick to at least say hello to us, but there was only dead silence. I was incredibly disappointed that Rick had left us holding the bag and put us in an unbelievably dire situation for months.

Jarrod spoke up immediately and took control of the conversation. He summarized the amount of debt we had incurred due to Rick's broken promises. Jarrod suggested to Rick's attorney that the fairest thing to do at that point was have Rick sign over the entire flock of sheep to us. Remembering our earlier conversation when Jarrod had said "He will never do it," I held my breath for the answer. Without hesitation, Rick responded, "Yes, I will sign them over now." Jarrod looked up with a look of surprise at Cliff and me, then agreed to fax over an official agreement for them to sign within the next five minutes. Before the call ended, Jarrod had one question that he politely asked Rick. "Why did you do this to Cliff and Deb?" With his voice breaking, Rick responded, "Because I wanted to say I owned that flock of sheep and be like them." With no further comments from Rick, not even an apology, Jarrod ended the conversation. Within five minutes, Jarrod faxed the agreement to them and it was immediately returned, fully signed by Rick. It was official. Cliff and I owned the entire flock. With my trust shattered by a man I had known for years, we never saw or heard from Rick ever again.

We were captive passengers on an emotional roller coaster. Our faith and trust had been broken and we found ourselves back to square one again. We were both back to performing jobs we did not want to be spending our lives doing. Out of necessity, we had to. We couldn't simply release the flock after dedicating so much of our lives to them, so we focused on raising money quickly to recover. The value was in the sheep, and although I did not want to part with any of them, I had no choice. If I could find a buyer for some of them, I could raise enough cash and still be able to attend the nationals.

I wasted no time in calling a farm in Virginia that had once purchased some of our top sheep. I presented the opportunity to Paul, the farm manager, to purchase 70% of the flock. He promised to get back to us after talking with the owner of the farm. I did not expect a call back for several days, but that evening, he called back with a counteroffer. He was willing to accept our offer, but only if Alpine, our stud ram, came with the group. Alpine was our only stud ram and a critical member of the flock. We did not intend to sell him; we needed him! It was an unexpected turn and one that I would have never agreed to, but I was backed into a corner. I felt Paul was taking advantage of our situation, and I hated the feeling of being pinched, but I had to agree. We planned to meet in Pennsylvania, which was over halfway, to make the transfer of our sheep to him.

Our sheep were like family to us, many of them having names. They were also a huge part of our history and legacy. Parting with them was heartbreaking. Our trailer was full as we pulled out of our driveway to make the long journey to meet Paul. We drove all night and met him at a truck stop parking lot in the wee hours of the morning. We backed both trailers up flush against each other to allow the sheep to walk into his trailer. I watched a good portion of my life walk away from me. It was an incredibly sad moment. Paul locked the door shut and handed me a check. I was happy that it was a cashier's check. Paul then stepped up close to my face, pointed his finger at me, and with a snide smile said, "Now we are going to kick your ass." His remark added insult to injury, leaving me speechless. I kept a positive attitude, thinking about how the upkeep of my remaining flock would be more manageable. We still had hope for good things to happen. Months later, Paul did actually defeat us. He won National Champion Ewe honors at the National Dorset Show and Sale held in Staunton, Viginia. Of course, it was with one of the lambs we raised that was on the trailer that night. We deposited the money for the sale and paid off the loan and all current bills. It was such a tremendous relief. Cliff had just been diagnosed with diabetes and would not be able to go to the nationals because he was not feeling well. Hannah was on the West Coast working, so she was not available. I had one of the strongest sets of sheep I had had in years, but I knew I could not go by myself. My 14-year-old neighbor, Lance, had shown great interest and enthusiasm in learning how to show sheep with me. I considered asking him if he would like to go. I telephoned his parents to ask if Lance could accompany me to Kentucky for the nationals and they immediately said yes. They passed the telephone to Lance. I asked him if he would like to accommodate me to the nationals and he was beside himself with excitement.

A few days later, we loaded up my best six sheep on the trailer, along with our cots, sleeping bags, and all the supplies we needed for the week. For the past twenty years, Cliff and I had always attended the shows together. It would be a first without him. With a lot of faith, prayer, and a full tank of gas, Lance and I began our 20-hour journey to Kentucky, arriving there barely awake.

The competition that year had a record number of entrants. However, I had confidence that the sheep we brought would be strong contenders. My sheep were penned next to the best in the country, some owned by multi-millionaires who had several employees on staff. There were many flocks from large universities backed by grants and donations from around the nation. I was there with my six sheep, a checkbook that could not afford a motel for the week, and a 14-year-old boy with little experience. However, we had big hearts and determination, and sometimes that is all you need. We tried to sleep by the sheep pens as the bright overhead lights stayed on all night and the night janitors cleaned hundreds of aisles in the barn with loud machine sweepers. It made for a short night for Lance and me. Hearing the crashing of the dumpsters being emptied into waste trucks all night cut into our sleep tremendously. The arena was filled with over 5,000 sheep, and many of them do not sleep at night. Sheep get bored and bang the feeders on their gates for hours, or butt heads with their neighbors. In the process, some of the stall gates were bent, allowing some of the sheep to escape and run around the barn exploring. Some of the exhibitors preferred to groom their animals at night, so there was loud music being played on beatboxes. If Lance and I got any sleep at all, it was because we passed out from pure exhaustion.

The next morning, one of my sheep reached through his gate and pulled on my sleeping bag, waking me up. I felt like I had not slept in days as I stumbled my way to the barn showers. I was facing an enormous amount of pressure to prove myself against the "big boys." Although I was operating on a shoestring budget, I always kept a pocket full of dreams and my faith held high. I was humbled when some of my good friends who were there from California and Texas offered to help us.

Five hours later, after many large classes all day long, my sheep placed consistently within the top three. I was grateful that we had a solid day. The last award to be presented was the highest award a breeder could win at the nationals. Awarded based upon a point system, it was given to the one breeder whose animals earned the most points by consistently placing the highest throughout the show. The recognition that came with winning that coveted achievement was a high reflection on not just one of your animals, but all of them. Photographers from nationally published sheep magazines were standing ringside waiting to take a photo of the winner. The announcer said, "This year's Premier Exhibitor Award was extremely close, with just a one-point difference between the two highest competitors. "This year's winner is Debby Jo Holmquist from Maine!" The other breeders swarmed in, congratulating me and embracing me from all directions. I felt an overwhelming sense of joy as my body shook with pure elation. The photographers stepped in to take photos of my best six sheep and Lance. My friends from California and Texas were right there with me. It was a moment in time, against all odds and then some. Two weeks earlier I was not even sure what the outcome of my flock would be, or if I could even afford to make the trip. With pride and gratefulness, Lance and I loaded up our precious six sheep to bring that elusive purple banner back home to Maine. The following week, I drove to Jarrod's office to show him the banner and give him the embroidered championship blanket that came with it. I told him a part of it belonged to him as well. Up until that day, I had never witnessed an attorney shed a tear.

Two weeks later, a letter arrived from Senator Susan Collins written on U.S. Senate letterhead from Washington D.C., congratulating me for my outstanding achievement of my win in Kentucky. She went on to say that she and the State of Maine were proud of me for representing the livestock industry so well. It was yet another reward for our perseverance and never giving up.

Premier Exhibitor Flock

2001 National Dorset Show-Louisville, KY

CHAPTER 32

As the Chair Turns

One of the greatest honors for a livestock breeder, is to be nominated by other breeders and subsequently contracted to serve as a professional judge. Over the past thirty years, I've held many judging positions on the east coast and received more requests from other regions. I was hired to judge a national breed show and sale at Penn State University, a large regional show in Seattle, Oregon, as well as a regional show in Baltimore, Maryland. I was contracted to judge a show in New Hampshire, Missouri, and Tennessee—all within the same week. During those three events, I evaluated over 1,000 sheep. I love judging shows and consider it a great honor. On my bucket list was to be invited to serve as a judge at the show where I won the Premier Exhibitor Award, and my dream came true!

I flew into Louisville the day before the show, readying for my task at hand the following day. The sheep shows were held in two large rings side by side in the convention center. The center was beautifully decorated with a bright white picket fence surrounding the show ring. The sheep were shown on specially dyed bright green shavings to give the appearance of elegance. The commentator introduced the judges just minutes before the show started. He pinned my judge's ribbon on my blouse and read my credentials. I listened proudly, but looking to my left, I saw a woman stand up and turn her chair so that her back was facing my ring. I thought to myself, *What an odd thing to d*o. The profile of the woman looked familiar. It was my mother!

I was stunned to see her at that event since I had never known her or my father to attend or compete there. Out of several rows of chairs facing the ring, her chair was the only one facing in the opposite direction. It was grossly obvious that she would not face my ring. After over twenty years, she still could not stand to look at me or acknowledge that her daughter had accomplished professional judging status. I was deeply saddened by her lack of respect in such a public venue during this significant moment for me. I glanced over to the ring of another judge and heard his wife bragging to those seated next to her. "That's my husband, I'm so proud of him," I heard her say. I thought about how great it would feel to have my parents whisper to someone next to them, "That's my daughter." I longed to hear those words but deep inside I knew I never would. It was a heart-wrenching moment of sadness wrapped in pain deep in my heart. With a quick scan of the crowd of the other spectators, I spotted my father seated far away. I kept my chin up while embracing the joyful task ahead of me for the day. I did not let my mother's humiliating act embarrass me or rattle my nerves. I performed my judging duties with professionalism and joy.

Only a handful of women have had the distinction of judging at the international show level. I am proud to say I was invited back to judge three more times and a fourth time as a panel judge in a national futurity competition. After that event, I never saw my parents again.

CHAPTER 33

In Sickness and in Health

In 2002, Cliff returned to the same company he had driven for until we left to move to the mountain farm. They were happy to have him back. He had been back driving for two months when I received a telephone call from his dispatch manager. He told me that Cliff was hauling a trailer full of cement dust and had been involved in an accident. Immediately, I called one of my friends to ride with me to the hospital three hours away. When we were a few miles from the New Hampshire hospital, we came upon the accident site. We saw his truck rolled over, lying on its side, the cab destroyed. Police cars were everywhere blocking off the highway by his truck. I gasped for dear life when I saw the condition of the truck and wondered how he could have survived it. When we arrived at the hospital, I ran straight to the emergency room where they were working on him. They assured me he would be okay but had suffered a concussion and multiple cuts and bruises. The paramedics who rescued him from the wreckage stated they had never seen a person come out of such devastation alive. They suspected his load of cement dust may have shifted as he was rounding a curve onto an exit ramp. This caused the trailer to completely roll over, pinning him and leaving him unconscious. The first responders had to cut the back of the cab off to extricate him. He remained unconscious for hours. I did not leave his side for the next four days until I could finally take him home to rest for a few weeks.

Cliff was diabetic, so what should have been a few weeks of recovery turned into a few months because his body had trouble healing. It was months before he could return to driving again. He had not been on the job long enough to earn any sick time, so my job was our only source of income. We were still supporting eighty head of sheep, and with our new farm mortgage, I had to secure a second job. After six months, Cliff had healed well enough to return to work. Five weeks after his return to work, I received another call from his best friend who drove for the same company.

"Hello, Deb? This is Dan. Did you hear about Cliff's accident?" My body fell limp.

"No, I haven't. What happened?" I nervously asked.

Dan explained that somehow Cliff's truck went off the road, rolling down a steep embankment where he was pinned for over two hours before another passing vehicle spotted him down in the valley. I was completely terrified for his well-being.

Cliff suffered fractures in his neck and a broken shoulder along with multiple cuts and bruises. He was taken 200 miles away, to the largest hospital in Maine to have surgery on his neck and shoulder. He needed metal fusions to be inserted. According to his doctors, it would take several months for him to recover. His diabetic condition caused his healing process to be dreadfully slow, and what should have been several months of recovery took several years instead. He needed an immeasurable amount of care. I did everything within my power before and after my workday to care for him. He was my priority, and I was willing to do whatever I had to do to get him well again. I adored him and was grateful he had survived two devastating accidents and was still with me. We both realized that his driving career was over, but it was not our first bump in the road. I had never realized what a monstrous and devastating disease diabetes is. Cliff and I were finding out the hard way.

Cliff developed an infection in his right foot that quickly spread, causing his right leg to swell to twice its normal size. I rushed him to the emergency room where he was admitted for a thirty-one day stay. The vascular disease caused by diabetes put him at severe risk of losing his entire right leg. He was fortunate to only have part of his foot amputated. He had a permanent PIC line inserted for the administration of antibiotics. His doctors wanted to admit him to a nursing home to continue his treatment. Because of my experience working at the farm and at the veterinary clinic, I was confident that I would be able care for him and treat his wounds at home. Cliff needed help with bathing, eating, and essentially all of his daily functions. I knew he would pull through; it was just going to take a lot of love, care, and a whole lot of faith and prayers.

For years, Cliff continued to struggle with diabetes and the pain from his accident injuries. Along the way he experienced many falls resulting from balance issues associated with the amputation. We had several pairs of special orthotic shoes made for him to provide relief, but he eventually had to rely on the full-time use of a walker. I was still maintaining our flock of sheep, and selling some individuals here and there to prospective breeders. My goal was to preserve the foundation flock to push forward once Cliff became better. Just when he would overcome his current infections, another one would appear, one after another, endlessly. We exhausted every treatment option. Despite our efforts, he couldn't overcome his ongoing infections and had to be admitted to the hospital over fifteen times. His doctor was adamant about admitting Cliff into a nursing home for further care, but I was even more determined that would not happen. Cliff's place was at home on the farm. I was committed to taking care of him right there. I would not break his heart and send him off for someone else to care for him. Because of his sedentary condition, he became quite angry and depressed. I was the only person he could take his frustration out on. One morning after I had bathed him and finished his wound treatments, he was so frustrated with me trying to keep his courage up that he said, "Why don't you just drop dead." I was crushed. I had dedicated every moment I had to care for him, and I was exhausted as well. On my drive to work, I couldn't control my emotions and had to pull over to sob uncontrollably. I was weary, and each time it seemed like we may be close to having a breakthrough, the disease kept throwing obstacles at us. Even with my two jobs, I could not earn enough income to sustain what we needed. We sold a few sheep here and there to support ourselves, the sheep, and cover the farm mortgage. There were not enough hours in the day for me to make it all work. Something had to give.

I had not been able to show our sheep for a while and I could barely maintain the expenses of their feed. Somehow, I had maintained their magnificent reputation. Some of the newborn lambs showed great promise, and that helped me continue to be hopeful. The hardest decision I had to make was to sell the last group of sheep. It was a matter of survival. There was a top breeder in Minnesota who had stayed in contact with me and occasionally inquired about purchasing the flock. He always asked me to keep him in mind if that day ever came. With excruciating pain, I lifted my telephone to inform him that the day had come. He was excited and honored that I was giving him the first opportunity to own the rest of my flock. We agreed on a final purchase price which would include everything—the sheep, their show blankets, my farm sign, and even my 32-foot-long aluminum sheep trailer. We made plans to meet in a few days at a truck stop in Ohio for the transfer. After I hung up from that call, my legs buckled underneath me as my body became limp from sheer sadness. It was the most gut-wrenching decision I have had to make in my life. With my arms folded on my desk, I laid my head down and sobbed until there was nothing left. In spite of all the obstacles I had overcome to keep my flock, I had finally reached the time when I had no choice but to let them go. Cliff came first, and thirty-three years earlier I promised him "in sickness and in health."

When the day arrived to load my remaining sheep, I removed our names from the farm sign and thought it would be a nice touch to add the new owner's name and address underneath our logo. I carefully slid it into a protective sleeve for transport. Cliff was too ill to accompany me on the 14-hour drive, so I prepared to make the final journey with my sheep alone.

I packed a couple of sandwiches and cold drinks in a small cooler set in the passenger-side seat. I embraced Cliff tightly, and held back my tears as I assured him, I would be back soon. The pain in his face was clear, as his eyes swelled with tears. I could barely see through the tears as I headed west on a trip I never expected I would have to make. I kept a good moderate speed, ensuring a safe ride for the passengers in my trailer as we made our way to Ohio. I was used to driving a truck and trailer on big roads, so was not afraid to drive. My only concern was staying awake for fourteen hours.

Coming closer to Columbus and driving through thick traffic, I was in constant communication with the new owner, keeping him informed of my location. As I pulled into the truck stop, he was there waiting for me with his huge dually truck. I could feel my body weaken from the thought of what was about to transpire. It felt like I had received a death sentence. We chatted for a few minutes, and I could tell he knew it was extremely difficult for me. He kept the conversation short and handed me a cashier's check in the full amount we had agreed on. With no words, we exchanged an embrace. I had words, but I could not get them out. I showed him the farm sign with his name on it and he was overwhelmed at my thoughtfulness. He pledged to keep me in the loop and proposed that I become his consultant later on. I eagerly accepted his offer. He was such a gentleman and unhooked my trailer. As I heard the safety chains drop from my truck and the cranking of the hitch up, I pulled my truck forward away from it. He connected everything back securely for his journey back to Minnesota, as I stood there, frozen. I watched my life drive away, listening to the "baas" of one of my favorite ewes. It was as if she were saying goodbye. I stood there until they faded from view — grief-stricken. Then I got myself into my truck because it felt like I was going to fall to the ground. I laid my head on the steering wheel and fell limp. Feeling like I had just lost my identity, I wondered, *How would I ever recover from such an empty feeling. Could I?* When I was unable to shed any more tears, because nothing was left, I pulled my truck over to a quiet spot in the corner of the truck stop. I passed out for a few hours before making the long journey home, alone, and without my sheep family in tow.

A year after that sorrowful exchange, Cliff was finally overcoming the enormous challenges he had faced. His favorite thing to do in life was driving a farm tractor to make hay in a hayfield. His best friend, Will, lived nearby with hundreds of acres that needed to be mowed and baled. He had orders to fill for horse and cattle customers needing their winter's supply of hay. Will needed additional help with the process and asked Cliff if he would like to assist. Cliff was feeling well enough and desperate to get out of the house, so he volunteered to help drive the tractor. After years of being couch-ridden, it was a tremendous opportunity for Cliff and would breathe new life into his spirit. He was extremely excited to get back to a normal life, and I was elated to see him smile again. His years of courage and determination were about to be rewarded. Cliff still required the use of his walker for help, but managed it well. He was able to drive himself the short distance to the hayfield and pull himself up onto the big farm tractor. The greatest pleasure for me was to witness the pure satisfaction on Cliff's face, doing what he loved. He spent several weeks helping Will under the warm summer sun, thoroughly enjoying himself. It was truly the best medicine he had received in years, besides being a tremendous help to Will. At the end of that day, Will threw fifteen bales of hay in the back of Cliff's truck to drop off to a local customer. That was a rewarding sight for Cliff, to be able look in his rear-view mirror and see the hay bales.

We had just received a telephone call from Hannah. She had not been home in several years, and reported she was going to have a few days off from her job out west. She wanted to come home to visit. Her fiancé, Juston, had never been to New England. Hannah wanted to bring him home to meet us and tour the state of Maine. When they arrived, we picked them up from the airport, and during our drive home, we planned a family day. I arranged to take a vacation day from work to join them. For the first time in many years, we would get to spend time together. It was a rare occasion.

Cliff was scheduled for a doctor's appointment the next morning. We planned to attend his appointment together, then travel to the mountaintop farm for old times' sake. We would show Juston where we invested an important part of our lives. We made it on time to Cliff's appointment at 9:00 a.m. After his examination, Cliff's lips trembled as he asked the doctor "Can I please turn in my walker, I don't want it anymore."

"You know, Cliff, I think this is the healthiest you have been in ten years. Yes, let's get rid of your walker today," he replied.

The reaction on Cliff's face was that of relief and victory. I spied a tear falling from the corners of his eyes. Cliff bragged to the doctor that his daughter and future son-in-law were visiting. The doctor said, "Go enjoy your day, you've earned this." I put my arm around Cliff as we happily exited his office. For the first time in years, he was able to walk out of the office without his walker. From there, we were off to enjoy our first day of freedom in what seemed like forever.

We hopped in the truck celebrating Cliff's milestone while heading to the mountaintop farm. The sun was shining brightly when suddenly a small rainstorm arose. The rainstorm was followed by the most magnificent bright rainbow I had ever witnessed. I glanced over at Cliff as I saw rays of sunshine shining through his window upon his shoulders. God had provided us with an angelic day. It felt like Cliff had just been blessed by the heavens in his new freedom. He pointed out his favorite hay field to Juston as we approached the farm. He said, "I loved to hay that field," as he smiled. Ordinarily, Cliff would have stayed in his truck while we got out and looked around. This time he enthusiastically stepped out with us. We all took in the glorious sights of the mountains and reminisced about our years spent there. We stopped in town at a small cafe and enjoyed a wonderful lunch while planning the next day's adventure. Juston had never seen the Atlantic Ocean, so we made plans to go there. Our little family enjoyed a glorious special day together catching up on years' worth of laughter and conversations. We spent the afternoon window-shopping in the small villages, and Cliff pointed out to Juston many of the tourist highlights.

We arrived home in time to enjoy dinner with Hannah's best friend, Amy, who stopped by to enjoy time with us. Of all Hannah's friends, Amy was Cliff's favorite. We all took part in making dinner together. Cliff laughed and joked with us as he joyfully partook in the preparation while showing us "the correct way" to cook. Normally, he did not show an interest in such things, so it was unusual for him. The kids drove to town to pick up snacks for our outing the next day. Cliff and I washed up the dinner dishes together and reminisced about the wonderful day we had all just spent together. Our hearts were filled with overwhelming love, joy, peace and happiness; something we had not experienced in quite a while. Our Hannah was there to share in our blessings, and all was right in our world.

Returning to his couch to watch television, I asked Cliff if he wanted a cold drink. "I would love to have some ginger ale," he replied. I promptly retrieved a glass for him and set it down on his tray. I remember looking at him lovingly and saying, "We had the best day together. You are my best friend and I would give my life for you. I love you so much." He gave me the same warm smile that he gave me on the day I met him. I saw a sparkle in his eyes that I had not seen in years. Our hearts were overflowing with gratitude.

One of Cliff's Truck Wrecks

CHAPTER 34

The Long Goodbye

Cliff and I were consumed with that moment of pleasure. Our lives were being restored, and our family was all together again. Suddenly, Cliff's head fell back with a blank look on his face, his eyes still. I thought he was playing a joke on me. His face quickly became white, his lips turned blue, and he was not moving or breathing. I kept rubbing his face while saying his name as I felt for a pulse. I could not feel anything! I dialed 911 as fast as my fingers could dial and begged the paramedics to please hurry as fast as possible. They assured me they would get to us momentarily. I hyperventilated through the shattering helplessness. I shook uncontroll-ably, feeling my heart thudding against my ribs trying to convince myself that it was not happening. *Please God, no.* I tried with all my strength to give Cliff CPR, but as his beautiful blue eyes faded, my instinct told me he was in big trouble. My front door flew open with five paramedics rushing to him with their equipment.

They placed Cliff on his back on the living room floor, cut off his shirt and began feverishly working on him. The lead paramedic was on the phone with the ER doctor, who guided him through the critical steps. After forty excruciating minutes the lead paramedic stood up in front of me and said, "I'm very sorry ma'am, your husband did not make it."

The shock was incomprehensible. His doctor had just told us that he was the healthiest he had been in ten years. Minutes later, the kids pulled into the driveway to witness utter shock and chaos. Juston assisted the paramedics in carrying Cliff out of the house as they placed his body in the funeral home van, quietly latching the door. I looked at the lead paramedic and said through my sobbing "You don't understand. You cannot take him. This is my best friend, and we have been married 33 years!" His sadness was palpable as he hung his head.

As the van slowly exited the driveway, Cliff's face was uncovered, and I could still see his blonde curls surrounding his lifeless face. I started running after the van to stop him. They were not supposed to be taking Cliff away from me. If I could catch the van, I would get Cliff back and everything would be okay. I ran faster after the van until Juston caught up with me and held me tightly in his arms. I tried to escape his grip until the van was out of sight. The trauma of that day caused unimaginable, tortuous pain. The next day, instead of enjoying the family vacation day we had planned, we were making Cliff's funeral arrangements. Despite being unfamiliar with the process, I had to persevere through the difficult task of selecting his burial garments, arranging a service to commemorate him, and deciding on his burial location. It was overwhelming. We later learned that Cliff had passed away the moment his head went back from what we believed was a blood clot.

At Cliff's service, I had never seen so many beautiful flowers in one place. They had been sent from around the country, from so many of Cliff's friends who adored him. The line of his friends, some whom had traveled hundreds of miles, went all the way from the funeral home door down the long sidewalk for a great distance. The deepest love and caring of friends was immeasurable. Cliff had a special ability to instantly befriend anyone. He was a caring, compassionate, and loyal soul to all. He never said a negative word about anyone, ever, and he exuded humbleness. He was happy-go-lucky and deeply treasured his family and friends. Cliff had a wonderful sense of humor and was always the social butterfly in the family.

A long-time family friend informed me that he had called my parents the day before the service to let them know about Cliff. According to him, their reaction was stone-cold. They lived only fifteen miles from me, but they were not in attendance. I received not a card, a call, flowers, or anything from them. During the darkest days of my life, they had an opportunity to reach out to me, but they did not.

Hannah, Juston, Amy, and our dear friend Mary followed the hearse to the cemetery riding in Cliff's pick-up truck still filled with those bales of hay just as he had left it. With each mile we traveled to Cliff's final resting place, I felt the pain cut deeper into my heart. Before his casket was lowered, I thought it was fitting to cut open one of the bales of hay on Cliff's truck and place some around the casket and the vault. It was something he loved, and it was part of nature that would surround him. His gravesite was on a soft hill that overlooked a farm belonging to one of his best friends. The farm was populated with cattle and sheep surrounded by a hayfield that you could see for miles. At the young age of 56, Cliff was resting in greener pastures.

Carloads of people followed us back to the farm to pay their respects. The outpouring of love was more than words could ever describe. Juston and Hannah had to catch a plane home back to the Midwest. My heart broke more to see them leave. I would be alone for the first time in thirty-three years. Hours had passed when the last visitor drove out of the driveway; it was almost dark with a chilling frost approaching. The damp musty orange and brown leaves of autumn were fluttering down from the trees onto my head and shoulders. I sat beneath the trees, unable to raise my chin because the pain of my grief was unbearable. I wanted nothing more than to be with Cliff. When I drove back to the cemetery, I walked over to his grave and collapsed facedown, sobbing inconsolably.

All sense of time had stopped, leaving a permanent hole in my heart. I did not think I would ever be the same person again. There was no escape from the dark, depressing, and exhausting days of grief. Grief is the stabbing mourning pain of yearning to get back what you have lost and realizing it will never be again. I had said goodbye to my treasured flock of sheep so I could devote all my time to Cliff. After saying goodbye to him, everything I loved and lived for was gone.

Cliff had been experiencing pain in one of his legs for several weeks that I kept telling his doctor about. The night before Cliff passed away, he experienced another severe episode of pain in the same leg that was so excruciating it brought him to tears. I told the doctor the morning of his last examination that he had experienced severe pain again, but the doctor did not address those symptoms. Just a few minutes before Cliff died, he told me his leg was quivering, but he brushed it off. I believe that his extended period of inactivity followed by physical activity, such as walking and climbing stairs, resulted in the dislodging of the clots in his leg. Sadly, one moved into his lungs, causing what we believed to be a massive pulmonary embolus (large clot to the lungs).

For several days, I could not answer any calls because of my dark emotional state. My friends' immeasurable friendship and love kept me going during dark days when I could finally answer their calls. The idea of parting ways with someone you've grown to love deeply and hold dear was beyond comprehension. It demanded immense strength, courage, and faith in God like never before. I spent my days in deep agony, with a broken heart and a spirit consumed by profound loneliness that clung to me like a heavy burden. Falling to my knees became a daily ritual at Cliff's grave. I crafted a red Christmas felt stocking for him on my first Christmas Eve without him. Christmas morning was also spent at his grave, kneeling over him, melting holes in the deep snow in front of me from my fallen tears.

Several weeks passed before I could bring myself to touch his favorite shirt, which still rested on his nightstand next to my bed. When I finally had the strength to pack away his clothes, I buried my face in that shirt and it still carried his scent. I crumpled onto the floor, sobbing with all my heart. Having only missed three days, I had to return to work to support my farm and cover Cliff's funeral costs. With no life insurance or savings in place, I put in extra hours of work at both of my jobs. On many mornings during my commute to work, I had to stop my car in a parking lot and cry because I missed Cliff so much. I spent a year and a half as a grief-stricken captive, crying myself to sleep every night. I pleaded with God to guide me on the right path. God works in mysterious ways; he has always answered my prayers.

CHAPTER 35

My Savior With Whiskers

Our dear friend Amy, who is a renowned veterinarian, telephoned me one morning. She wanted to let me know that someone had abandoned a box of kittens on her doorstep in the dark of the night. They were adorable, frightened, cold and hungry. I imagine whoever did it must have known Amy would find them suitable homes. She asked me if I would like one of the kittens, and of course, I said yes! Later that day, she delivered a precious little black and white kitten weighing less than four pounds riding on her shoulders. He was the classic tuxedo kitty, with four white mittens, a white bib-like chest with a white bowtie nose accentuated by thick long white whiskers. His dark green eyes vividly expressed his emotions. He was perfect. She passed him to me and I felt an immediate deep connection. I lovingly named him Kitty Pie. I took him to bed with me the first night. He laid on my chest licking my face as if to say, "Thank you." If he only knew how much he was saving my soul; I was the one who needed to be thanking him instead. We both desperately needed love and security, and God arranged for our needs to be met.

He was exactly what I needed to help break up the extreme loneliness I felt at night. Kitty Pie knew when I was sad and would always cuddle closer to me, many times licking the tears off my cheeks. He was my grief counselor, my best friend, and my faithful loyal companion. His way of distracting me to play with him constantly resulted in joy and laughter. His mischievousness provided me a start to healing.

Fifteen years later, Kitty Pie and I are still inseparable best friends. Over time, he grew and weighed eighteen pounds, consisting solely of pure quintessence. He never missed a night sleeping beside me, with his soothing purring because he was content. When he and I were together, I was also content.

My Savior Kitty Pie

CHAPTER 36

My Journey Back to Life

I had spent a good part of the last eleven years taking care of Cliff. After undergoing many doctor's visits and multiple hospital stays, my interest in the medical field developed. I wanted to make a positive difference because there were too many unpleasant office visits. I wanted to do it in Cliff's honor, so that perhaps the next patient would feel more compassion rather than being looked upon as a number.

I received a college course booklet one day in the mail offering nationally certified medical classes. I thought it would be a wonderful opportunity for me to learn something new and make a difference in this world. I would have to pay for the classes, purchase my books, and travel two hours after work for the evening classes. The classes would cost over $4,000, but I decided to sign up and do it. I was excited to set a goal to better myself and do something new that would keep my mind occupied.

I spent the next two years in class learning medical terminology, medical billing and coding, electronic medical records and medical office administrative assistance. Some of my classes started with twenty students and as the weeks progressed, even though their employers were paying for their classes, over half of the students dropped out. One of my classes ended with only three students left. The classes were long and grueling with hours of homework and studying required. I took an interest in learning and studied hard for all the exams. In the medical terminology class, we were assigned to do a presentation of a medical case of our choosing. I chose the dreaded disease of diabetes as I had first-hand experience of the horrid effect it has on people. I spent weeks preparing large colorful three-dimensional visual charts and handouts. I was proud of the work I had done and I thought of Cliff during all of it.

After the final presentation and grades, I won the award for the most outstanding and educational submission. I was truly humbled that the professor requested I leave my presentation with her to use for future class references. That was an immensely proud moment for me and gave me hope that it would help others in need in the future. I completed all four classes, graduating with top honors and national certifications in each. As I left the building with my certificates, I looked up at the sky and said, "These are for you, Cliff."

Three years after losing Cliff, I had learned grief's lesson from the passage of time. I learned how to embrace the lessons and allow them to strengthen me. My spirit could not let grief dominate my life. It was up to me to align myself and come back to life, relying on my inner strength and determination. I accepted the challenge to create a new life and get up again because I realized that no one else could do it for me.

My mind reawakened to restore my passion for raising and showing sheep. I wanted to live, not just exist. Hannah was living in Illinois, in luscious farmland and great sheep country. It was a known fact that some of the best sheep in the nation were raised in Illinois. Hannah occasionally gently suggested that I could move there, live near her, and start a new life. The idea floated around in my mind for quite a while. If I moved to Illinois, I would be close to all the large shows and would not have to drive over 1,000 miles to get to them. I would be in the middle of sheep country amongst many top breeders, and I would be closer to my family. Something was calling me to head West. It would be a monumental decision because, after all, Maine was the only home I had ever known. I had spent 55 years of my life in Maine and I loved it. I had two good jobs that I had worked at for years and had many long-time friends around me.

I felt it was time to embrace life's adventure and open my arms to fulfill my destiny. I had faith that God would steer me in the right direction. My thirty-acre farmland, including the 150-foot barn, required a tremendous amount of maintenance. There were not enough hours in the day for me to maintain it while holding down two jobs. My back injury from my fall years earlier was raising its ugly head and the pain was getting worse. I received a call one morning from Hannah informing me she and Juston had driven by "the cutest little farm" close to them. It had a for sale sign on it! She thought it would be perfect for me. I felt like it was a sign, so I flew out to Illinois for a quick weekend trip to investigate the little farm. It was a small but charming 750 square foot old farmhouse, over one hundred years old and surrounded by six acres of beautiful pasture. It was fenced with old sheep wire fencing and had a small barn on the back of the property. It was calling my name! I phoned the realtor right away to express my interest. I explained that I needed to sell my farm back in Maine, but meanwhile, I was going to try to secure the place. He referred me to a local banker in town who specialized in farm loans. The place needed a lot of work and upgrades, but I knew it was a place that was meant for me.

CHAPTER 37

Let's Begin Again

I flew back home the next day feeling a sense of newness and purpose. That Monday morning, I telephoned the banker, and was faxed a farm loan application which I immediately completed. That afternoon, he telephoned me to inform me my loan was approved! My farm in Maine sold quickly to a nice family that owned several racehorses. After the settlement of the sale, I used the funds to pay for my new farm in full and had extra funds available to purchase some sheep again!

The impending move became a reality. I was leaving the place Cliff and I called home and had planned to spend the rest of our days. I strolled through the farm, gazing at the special trees we had planted together, the new front door, and the steps we saved money to purchase. The rose bushes we planted together gracefully rested by the front steps in full, red, fragrant blossoms. I took down our farm sign, which was hanging over a wooden handmade water well we constructed, to bring it along. I visited the cemetery to say goodbye to Cliff. There would be no more daily visits. I carefully planted several daffodil bulbs around his grave, ensuring a yearly reminder of my presence. I fell to my knees one last time spilling puddles of tears as they absorbed in the dirt. In the past, when it was time for us to load up our sheep and head to a show, he would always say, "Get your ass in the truck and let's go." Weakened by the thought of me leaving, I mustered up the strength to stand, and said, "Get your ass in the truck, you're going with me." My heart was heavier than a load of bricks as I left that sacred ground one last time. Cliff would always be in my heart—I keep him there.

With the help of my friends, we packed the large U-Haul truck so full there was no room for a piece of paper to slide in. My dear friend, Dana, from New Hampshire and I were ready to make the long drive to Illinois from Maine. I will forever be grateful to him for his kindness and friendship in my great time of need. With my best friend Kitty Pie in his carrier, I climbed into the U-Haul and said goodbye to Maine with God's winds beneath us.

It was a grueling 30-hour drive in a behemoth truck that was so loud you could not hear yourself think. The seats were narrow and hard, and I felt excruciating pain in my back with every bump we hit. The weather was brutally hot, and halfway through our trip, the air conditioner broke. We rolled down the windows as sweat rolled down our faces, and Kitty Pie screamed most of the way.

When we finally reached our destination, Hannah, Juston, and some of their friends were awaiting our arrival at the new little farm as we drove in. They unloaded the truck in record time and placed my belongings in a pile in the middle of the living room floor. Kitty Pie was happy to inspect each room, investigating all the unfamiliar smells and adjusting perfectly. The long ride exacerbated my back pain, which brought me to tears. Hannah made a telephone call to a well-known local chiropractor who agreed to see me the next morning. With each step I took towards his office, the pain became unbearable. I ended up sitting on the exam table, in tears, clearly in a terrible state. The doctor immediately ordered a STAT MRI on my back, and we drove two hours to the hospital to have it done. Two days later I underwent a laminotomy and discectomy for ruptured disks in my spine. When I awoke from the surgery, I felt immediate relief from the pain. However, the ruptured disks had been sitting on nerves so long, I lost most of the feelings in my right toes permanently. I was still grateful for the relief and got myself up and going the next day. The surgeon advised me to rest for several weeks, but I needed to get a job to sustain myself. What a way to start my new life in Illinois!

With medical certifications under my belt, I applied at a large hospital thirty miles away and was hired on the spot. I started the following week at the full-time job I had landed working in the urology clinic. I was on my way!

Months had passed and I was still settling into my new farm in the Midwest. The old sheep fence already in place had random gaping holes in it, and because of its age it was not repairable. It was not sufficient for security to keep the sheep in and predators such as coyotes and dogs out. It needed to be repaired before I brought any sheep onto the property. In my younger years, we lost forty-five sheep in one day from an attack by four stray dogs: a devastating loss to any sheep farmer. Sheep are defenseless animals whose only recourse is to run, so a secure, tight fence was a necessity.

I contracted a local Amish fence company that had a stellar reputation to put in a new fence around the entire property. It was a task that normally would take a few days, but the crew came in with ten young men and had it up in one day. They did a masterful job which was worth the $10,000 investment. They installed the entire fence and the extra gates I brought with me from Maine to divide pastures as well.

I spent days repairing a few leaky roof panels, sweeping dusty cobwebs off the rafters and walls, washing the windows, and trimming the overgrown weeds away from the barn. My back was still healing and tender, but my determination was strong to get everything set up to accommodate my new sheep. Bagged shavings to use as bedding for the sheep were quite expensive. I was trying to save every penny, so I took my old truck and drove twenty miles over to the next town to a sawmill that had free sawdust for the taking. It saved me a lot of money, but I had to load it myself. I shoveled sawdust for over three hours, one shovel full at a time, onto my truck bed. Every few shovels full, I stepped up into the pile to pack it down, trying to fit as much as I could. Once home, I took one shovel full at a time, spreading it by hand around the floor in the sheep pens until it was a few inches thick. It took several more hours of back-breaking work, but when I was finally done, it looked and smelled fresh, like ground up pine trees. Fresh clean bedding is a necessity for livestock health, so I repeated that process every month, year-round so that my sheep would have "fresh sheets."

I drove thirty miles to the nearest grain store to stock up on bags of grain. I purchased what is called "show feed," a special recipe that contained only high-quality grains infused with high-quality minerals and vitamins. The cost of each bag was double the cost of regular grain, but my theory was to provide the best quality feed to achieve the best results. In my opinion, the sheep would only be as good as what they were fed. The grain store employees loaded the fifty-pound bags of feed in my truck for me, but I had to unload it. I could not lift the bags, so I slid one bag at a time back to the tailgate, opened the top, and hand scooped as much as I could carry into a bucket, then carried each bucket full to the feed barrel. If I had been able to lift the bag of grain, I could have completed that chore in minutes. Instead, it took me a considerable amount of time.

I used hot, soapy water to wash the water buckets I had used for my last group of sheep in Maine so the new sheep would always have fresh access to water. There was another sheep breeder who lived just a few miles from me with several hundred bales of hay stacked in his barn. I drove over to his place to ask if I could purchase five bales from him.

"No!" was his unfriendly answer. He was a competitor, and I do not think he was pleased about me moving into his territory. Instead, I traveled fifty miles to a hay auction and purchased twenty-five bales. The auction crew stacked it in my truck for me, but I also had to unload them myself. Each bale weighed approximately seventy pounds, so I pulled a bale off the truck and rolled it, one at a time, into the barn. That was yet another task that took me hours each week, constantly testing my back healing.

For my first winter in Illinois, we had a bad snowstorm with snow as high as my hips. I had a ewe that had just delivered babies, and I had been up most of the night with her, ensuring her lambs were going to be okay. Only half a bale of hay was left. Being unable to drive to the hay auction because of the blizzard, I was desperate to get some good quality alfalfa hay to give her. I pushed my pride aside and reluctantly drove back to the place where the crusty old man had told me "No" earlier. I hoped maybe he had a change of heart and would sell me one bale to get me by until I could go get a load at the auction. Because there was such a severe storm, my hopes were high that he would show some compassion. I walked tentatively in the knee-deep snow and knocked on his door. He barely cracked open the door as I tenderly explained my situation. I asked, "Is there any chance I could buy just one bale of hay from you to get me by?" With narrowed eyes and an ugly twist to his lips, he replied "No, I don't think so." I thanked him anyway and walked away with disappointment, thinking to myself, "He is certainly not going to win the award for being neighborly."

The physical labor of running my farm was demanding. The sheep required shearing each spring to keep them cool in the summer months. Their feet needed trimming every few weeks along with worming, vaccinating, and all the particular care the baby lambs required. You must have a strong body to manage big sheep; a strong back, and a lot of courage. Some days, life overwhelmed me. There was never an extra penny for anything that I needed, let alone what I wanted. I lived week to week with my paychecks, ensuring first I always had feed for my sheep. Some days, my body would weaken and collapse on a bale of hay, my heart and body depleted. I hated the term "widow." But I felt the extreme loneliness of not having Cliff to share life with, to encourage me, and to love me. I hated those feelings and prayed that the wrenching, aching feelings would fade away. Even though I was feeling sorry for myself, I kept reminding myself to stand back up and dig deeper. There was never any downtime. Farming is not for the weak of heart, especially when raising livestock.

In the best of circumstances, some sheep died, even when all avenues to save them had been exhausted. It was always devastating to the heart, not to mention the economic loss. I have had my share of losses that kicked my heart to the curb, but as in anything in life, death is a given. It takes every ounce of courage to raise your chin and continue.

During lambing time, I would get out of bed twice a night during the freezing cold to check for newborns. It was important for me to be present to ensure their survival, especially on the brutally frigid winter nights. The leading cause of death in newborn lambs is hypothermia and starvation. They must receive colostrum from their mothers immediately to protect them with antibodies that fend off intestinal and respiratory diseases. Colostrum also reduces loss from hypothermia while providing them with energy and nutrients. If they do not receive that within the first twenty-four hours of life, they most likely will not survive. When my lambs were born in especially freezing weather, I automatically stripped healthy doses of colostrum from the mother and within minutes stomach tubed the baby lambs with it, so I knew they had a positive jump start to life.

It was tough getting out of my warm bed to face the wind, which was so cold it cut through my body. I made my way, half asleep, to the barn, but once I got there and saw healthy newborns, it was all worth it. Many times, if the lambs were breached, I had to assist mothers in delivering them. I have delivered thousands of lambs in my lifetime as a shepherd, but it never gets old. Hearing the first tender "baa" of a newborn lamb always warms my heart and brings a smile to my face. Just knowing that I had a part in helping to bring that life into the world is everything. Some mornings after arriving at the hospital, I would think to myself, *If these people in my office only knew what I was doing two hours ago.* Just hours before, I was up to my shoulder inside a ewe turning a lamb during a difficult birth with amniotic fluids all over me. I was kneeling with my face up against the mother's rear, getting to know her really well while assisting her delivery. I led two separate lives.

I worked at that hospital for a few years and had a perfect attendance record. I had also won "Employee of the Month" a few times. The doctors I worked for were kind and supportive and affectionately nicknamed me "Sheep." Patients would have a puzzled look on their faces when the doctors said, "Sheep, pass me their chart" or "Sheep, call radiology and schedule a STAT CT," or "See Sheep on your way out to schedule your next appointment." My hospital job required an enormous amount of my time and energy, but it was a job I needed to support myself and my sheep dreams. When the next spring arrived, I received some exciting news in the mail.

CHAPTER 38

On the Road Again

I was elated when I went to my mailbox on a spring day and saw a notice that there was a large sheep sale being held in Ohio. I thumbed through the catalog, studying the entries, and the name of the offspring I sold right before Cliff passed, caught my eye. When I saw that name, it was the motivation I needed to get ready to get back on the road to show my new Illinois flock. In preparation, I took out a loan to purchase a new livestock transport trailer and painted my new farm name on it. In neon green and black paint, the name "Show Girlz Sheep Company" was displayed. Cliff always liked the chrome burlesque showgirls that truckers put on their 18-wheeler mud flaps, so I thought he would have liked the new name and theme.

I traveled to Ohio with my new trailer in tow and walked into the sheep arena feeling like my life had returned to me. I took deep breaths, inhaling all the wonderful barn smells of hay, shavings, grain, and, of course, the sheep. I saw old friends I had not seen in years and was deeply touched by the "welcome back" embraces. I made my way to the pen where the daughter of my former sheep was stalled. Her pedigree was on a stall card hanging over her, showing my name under her mother's pedigree. It was a surreal moment that was meant to be. I examined her closely and saw that she was a gem of a specimen. She was eight months old, the perfect age to show for the next two years. She was an excellent size for her age. I was pleased that she was structurally outstanding and carried that beautiful breed type I had worked to instill in my breeding lines for years. I was instantly in love and set my heart to bring her home. As she walked into the auction block, bids began flying furiously from the crowd. I had decided she was coming home with me, so I kept raising my trembling hand until finally, the auctioneer slammed the hammer down, "SOLD!" She was mine!

It was a very emotional moment. I was flying solo, relying on my inner strength and courage for an incredibly challenging journey ahead of me. I needed to prove to myself that I could achieve greatness once again. I asked myself, *Am I dreaming too big? Can I really do this again starting at ground zero? Many breeders have years of success built ahead of me; can I catch up?* I could not afford to allow doubt or fear to quench my determination. I had just purchased my first sheep derived from my bloodlines in order to start over once more. No one could convince me that was not God's plan for me that day. I named her "Gem" as that is exactly what she was to me. That day I also purchased five other pregnant females that were due to give birth later in the fall.

That evening, when I returned home and observed my new sheep stepping onto my land, I experienced a deeply proud moment. I sat quietly in the barn gloating over them as they sniffed around their new home, munching on luscious green alfalfa hay. Looking up to the heavens as I left the barn, I thanked God for restoring my soul and bringing me back to what I loved most.

Over a year passed as I patiently and strategically planned my future with my new flock. I continued to add one or two sheep here and there when I could afford it. Another breeder, who was close to me and also a competitor, had some females to sell. I purchased the best one out of his group for $3,000. That amount was a lot of money for me at the time, but I wanted to show goodwill by supporting a local breeder. He was a member of the Dorset sheep association in my area, so I immediately joined as a new member. The association was contracted for a two-page advertisement to be printed in a national sheep magazine highlighting all the local breeders. I asked to be included in the ad. I wanted to announce to the other breeders around the country that I was in Illinois and introduce my new farm name. Two weeks later, much sooner than I expected, I opened my mailbox and there sat the national magazine. While anxiously thumbing through it, I saw the full two-page advertisement for the association highlighting all the Illinois breeders. My heart sank that my submission had not made it in time to be printed. I immediately phoned the other breeder to ask him why I had not received the information I needed in order to place my ad in the magazine. He replied, "Oh, I forgot you were here." Well, he had not forgotten to cash my $3,000 check I had given him two weeks earlier! That was my "Welcome to Illinois." I felt like a true outsider.

Later, I received a flyer in the mail with the schedules for the national shows and sales for the next three years. They rotated each year to a different state. In three years, the National Dorset Show and Sale was going to be held in Illinois! I taped the schedule to the front of my refrigerator and set a goal to attend. Three years seemed like a long time, but I needed that time to rebuild my bloodline. Each of the five pregnant ewes I purchased the year before produced top-notch quality lambs, and I was thrilled that they showed great promise. I had attended no shows for many years and yearned to return again.

I watched the new lambs mature over the summer and felt they would be excellent contenders in the upcoming state fair competition. Many of the best breeders in the Midwest would compete. I was apprehensive about how I would be accepted as a New England outsider. When I drove into the fairgrounds to unload my sheep, the assigned pens for me were far away from the show ring. I took it in stride, seeing that the locals were penned close to the show ring. I expected to be treated as the low man on the totem pole. Some competitors were not friendly or welcoming. In all the years I had shown, I always stayed humble and never hurt anyone or cut corners to get to the top. On show day, I won 4th and 5th place with my two ewe lambs. It was a good start for me. I got my feet wet again and returned home with my focus on preparing for the nationals which would be held that fall. After a thirteen-year absence from the nationals, I was excited to pay my entry fees to attend.

After months of anxiously waiting, I was back at the most prestigious livestock show in the world in Louisville with two ewe lambs that I raised from birth. They had grown well over the summer, and I was grateful and happy to be there amongst the greatest sheep in the land. Joyce, one of my longtime dear friends who had also moved to Illinois, was at the show. She was a lifelong professional sheep showman and fitter. We both grew up in New England and had known each other since we were teenagers. She was among the most talented at her skills in the nation. I was grateful to have her assist me in fitting my sheep for the competition. It was a successful day; my lambs won first and second place! The last class of the day was called the "Best Headed Award," which was an important award to receive. It was given to only one sheep that best represented her breed in overall beauty and breed type. A beautiful large walnut perpetual plaque with the breeder's name engraved on a gold plate was awarded each year. My name was on that plaque three other times from my Sugarloaf days, and it would be a dream to win it again. I entered my ewe lamb "Callie," into that class competition. She had won her class that day and had received multiple compliments on her outstanding breed type throughout the show. I knew from the day she was born that she "had that look about her."

There were many beautiful entries, and I watched as the judge walked up and down the line several times as each handler held their sheep's head high, making sounds or gestures for them to perk their ears so they looked picture perfect. Suddenly, the judge stopped at me and Callie and outstretched his hand to shake mine and awarded us the plaque. I was overwhelmed with pride and joy. Thirteen years later, my name would be engraved on the plaque once again. Soon after I returned home, I designed a new slogan to put on my farm sign that read, "Home of the pretty ones."

CHAPTER 39
The Morals of the Story

It was my third year living in Illinois. I kept some of the new lambs to add as foundation females to my growing flock which had grown to twenty-five sheep. It was time to add a stud ram to breed with my females. As luck would have it, one of the best breeders in the nation from Oregon was selling her flock. She posted a photo of a young ram she was going to sell first. As soon as I saw his photo and read his bloodlines, my jaw dropped at the possibility of owning him. It was a unique opportunity to add a vital piece of out-cross genetics to my flock, but I knew I did not have enough money to purchase him. Thinking of a way to raise some cash quickly, I remembered a beautiful handmade silver belt buckle embedded with red rubies and emeralds that I won years ago. If I sold it, it might bring enough for me to purchase that ram. I did not want to let it go, but I knew I would always have the memory of winning it. Besides, it was just sitting in a case. I justified selling it by telling myself that I could use that award to turn it into something bigger. I took my special buckle to an upscale jewelry store where they put it under a gemological microscope to verify the gemstones and the silver. They offered me less than what it was worth. With what I received along with working overtime, I was able to buy the stud ram. When I phoned to see if the ram was still available, it was!! I quickly spoke for him, and she was happy that he was going to be an integral part of my flock.

My new stud ram was on his way to my farm from Oregon. He was being transferred onto three different trailers in ten days to make the connection to Illinois. After traveling 2,200 miles, my stud arrived. All my hopes for the future were riding on him. When I gazed into the side of the trailer to look at him, my jaw dropped in amazement at how impressive he was. He weighed over three hundred pounds, but was muscular, strong, and heavy-boned on his feet and legs. He was the epitome of a stud ram. I reached my hand in and gently stroked his head thinking he would like a pat, but he firmly stomped his foot while snorting at me mad as a bull!

Along with his extraordinary good looks, he had a nasty, larger-than-life attitude! Not all sheep are nice, and some, especially rams, can be mean. I named him "Mr. Oregon."

Mr. Oregon settled in nicely. I immediately put him to work in my flock to produce unique bloodlines as outcross genetics to my females. He was mature enough to breed forty females easily. One fall evening during the breeding season, the blazing orange and pink sunset had just graced my little farm with darkness falling soon. I took a stroll in the pasture to check on Mr. Oregon and the brood ewes. Sometimes it felt good just to be a part of their peace and serenity. As I walked amongst them, petting their sweet heads, I noticed Mr. Oregon was standing further down the pasture with another ewe. Suddenly, I saw him lift his head high and stomp his foot hard on the ground in anger. He snorted like an angry bull and began running towards me in a fast and furious gallop. I turned and ran as fast as my legs could carry me towards an exit gate that was about one hundred feet away. The gate was latched shut, and I knew I would not have time to stop and open it. I heard his large strong hooves pounding the ground and knew he was on a mission to do me bodily harm. In that live or die moment, I quickened my pace another notch and hurled myself up and over that four-foot-high gate. As I was pulling my last leg up and over the aluminum gate, he head-butted it so hard he dented the gate. As I fell over it to safety, he continued to butt the gate to be sure I knew he was there. He was extremely angry that I was in with his ewes. He was going to make sure I left his territory. I got the message to never come to his pasture again while he was with ewes!

It was a narrow escape that evening and I was grateful for my speed and agility to fly over the gate. Mr. Oregon was a ram that you never wanted to turn your back on, or he would take advantage of the situation and could cause significant injury. He damaged many of my gates and feeders, pounding them to pieces with his "worldly attitude" which is typical for some stud rams. From the moment he arrived at the farm, I knew he was going to be a high-maintenance ram, but if he sired good lambs, I was willing to put up with him. I was counting the days until spring arrived to see what his lambs would look like and I prayed they would be as good as I hoped. His first baby lambs appeared with breathtaking results. His lambs were large, structurally correct, and exhibited the most beautiful breed type I had ever seen. There was one ram lamb born in February on a frigid wintry night during a snowstorm at two in the morning. I had to assist with his delivery as his mother, being a first-time lamber, needed help. After some patient work between his mother and me, I delivered him into this world. He was so impressive that I physically gasped when his entire body was out. A normal lamb weighs between 7 to 12 pounds; he tipped the scales at 18! I dried him off with a warm towel and wiped his face clean, revealing the prettiest face I had ever seen on a newborn lamb. My joy was palpable. I named him "Moxie" which means courage or determination, grit, or gumption, and I thought that name was appropriate. Moxie's first "baas" were very meek and the sound of his voice melted my heart. I watched as his mother softly murmured back to him as they bonded. That was my reward. I spent most of that night in the barn watching his mother lovingly accept and care for him.

Several more of Mr. Oregon's stunning offspring arrived, propelling my spirits to the heavens. They were indeed exquisite, and I could see that my plan was working. As the summer progressed, Moxie was maturing into a beautiful show sheep, and better yet, a stud ram. I exposed another set of my best females to him for breeding once he was six months old. I had big plans to show Moxie at the nationals that November. When other breeders visited my farm that summer, I heard many comments like, "He will be the one to beat." The competition was a few months away, and I was extremely excited to prepare him for entry.

One morning as I was feeding the sheep, I noticed Moxie was not standing at his feeder waiting for his breakfast. He was always the first in line to eat, so I knew something must have been wrong with him. I looked around in the pasture and there he was, lying down. I immediately took his temperature and, although he had no fever, he was grinding his teeth and straining to urinate. Those were telltale signs he did not feel well. I ran to the house to call the veterinarian. He was located two hours away, and I requested he come as soon as possible to look at Moxie. After the doctor examined him, he determined Moxie had a severe case of kidney stones (urinary calculi), a common metabolic disease in male sheep. He prescribed plenty of fluids, antibiotics and pain medication, which I administered faithfully, morning and night. After several days, Moxie was still not improving. The vet suggested a very expensive surgery as an option for Moxie, which I planned to have done immediately. That evening at feeding time, as I was readying his medications, Moxie passed away right in front of me. I was devastated. He was one of the best sheep I had ever raised. I was three months away from taking him to the nationals, where I felt he would have made his mark, but it did not happen for me that year. Another gut-wrenching, devastating blow. My heart was broken by the loss. All I could do at that point was pray that by the following spring I would have some of his lambs on the ground to carry his bloodline forward. It was a long, anxious wait.

The bitterly frigid winter months of the spring followed. My anticipation was extremely high, hoping for some new Moxie lambs to be born. Sure enough, every single female I had exposed him to, had begun to show big bellies. In early February, with the thermometer reading an even zero degrees, my best ewe, Fantasy, was in labor for the first time. I told myself I would not leave her side, no matter what. I had a warm nursery pen ready for her, bedded with deep golden straw and a warm heat lamp hanging overhead to take off the winter chill. She was extremely uncomfortable for a couple of hours until finally, she laid down to push.

I did not want to interfere unless I needed to, so I let her progress as much as she could until it was obvious she needed some help. She turned her head toward me with her large soft brown eyes, looking grateful for some help. Sliding on my delivery sleeves past my elbows, I could feel the lamb was presenting the right way with its head tucked in between its front legs. With each push Fantasy made, I gently pulled the two front legs with one hand and cupped the back of the lamb's head with my other hand. Showing great patience, I slid the lamb out after a few tense minutes. Once it was completely out, I gasped at the size of it. It was a ram lamb that took my breath away. Barely fitting on the lamb scales, it weighed twenty pounds! He was heavy-boned and adorned with the prettiest head and a bright rose-pink nose. He was a perfect specimen for a Dorset lamb. My limbs trembled with excitement! I had a special name already picked out for the first male born out of Moxie. I named him Morals.

Morals-2018 National Champion Ram
Bred and Raised by Debby Jo

CHAPTER 40

Creating a Masterpiece

More beautiful Moxie lambs arrived in the coming days, and I was blessed with a beautiful strong lamb crop. As the weeks passed, they showed great signs of becoming show sheep in their growth, development, and eye appeal. A potential show lamb will gain well over a half a pound a day for the first one hundred days of their life. The new lambs were right on target while maintaining great body structure along the way. The last lamb born that month was a single ewe lamb who looked identical to Morals in her size and appearance, yet she had the perfect feminine appearance with a dainty head. She tipped the scales at seventeen pounds, which was especially large for a female. I named her Ruby after my favorite gemstone and also my birthstone.

A good shepherd understands the fundamental principles of animal nutrition, its functions, and the importance of vitamins and minerals. They also understand the necessity of the proper quality and quantity of protein in their rations. Sheep love cracked corn, soybean meal, sweet oats covered in molasses, and high-quality green leafy alfalfa hay, which is high in protein. I wanted to try a new brand of grain I had heard about, which was specifically made for show sheep. I had done some research and found that it had an excellent reputation. It was expensive, but I thought it would be worth the investment. Another competitor, who was over eighty miles from me had become a dealer, so I ordered my first few bags of grain from him. I drove over eighty miles, one way, to pick it up at his warehouse and the lambs loved it. I was impressed by their performance and continued to order a few bags each week.

As the entry deadline for the nationals approached, I planned to enter my two best lambs, Morals and Ruby. A month away from the competition, I made my weekly trip to the grain dealer to pick up my order. I backed my truck up to the loading dock and eyed the dealer walking out to meet me. "Sorry, Deb. I forgot to order your grain. I'll have it for you next week." I was devastated! Maintaining consistency in a feeding program was critical because sudden changes to the feed disrupts the digestive system of sheep. The grain was a special recipe that could not be purchased anywhere else. It left me in a bad lurch, especially since it was so close to showtime.

The dealer assured me that my order would be in the following week. I waited until then and made another 80-mile trip to his loading dock to pick up my order. I had a sinking feeling when I saw him step out of the warehouse and approach my truck with a smirk on his face. "Sorry, Deb. I forgot your order again and I don't have any left." At that moment I realized and accepted the fact that forgetting my order was a competitor's way of saying, "I'm not going to help you." I got the message loud and clear. Sadly, I returned to my farm empty-handed and feverishly got to work to find a new grain dealer to purchase from. I was able to find another reliable source for grain. Carefully, I introduced the new feed to my sheep, praying that they would not show any negative results or weight loss from the sudden change of feed. My lambs adjusted well to the new diet, and we were ready to head to Kentucky for the nationals.

I proudly had both of my first "Moxie" lambs in place, ready for the competition that was a few days away. It was important to get the sheep settled in for a show a few days ahead of time to let them adjust to their new surroundings and rest from the trip. I also needed a few days of preparation time. I was immensely proud of them, especially since they were the second generation of the bloodlines I had created. I could hardly wait to see how they would compare to the other great sheep that were competing.

When competition day arrived, Morals was my first entry for the day. I walked him calmly for a few minutes before entering the show ring and he behaved nicely. Other breeders complimented him as I passed by heading toward the show ring. I could have an assistant in the ring to help me, so my friend Joyce joined me. Morals was impressive standing beside the other competitors, but just like his daddy, he exhibited a temper. He disliked the other ram lambs standing beside him and threw a tantrum in the ring. Joyce and I did everything possible to keep him calm and under control, but he would not have any part of behaving that day. The judge got tired of waiting for him to stand still, so that landed him in fifth place. He was good enough to win the class, but I understood the judge's thinking as he just could not get a good look at him to carefully evaluate him. Fifth place at the nationals was very respectable, but I had to wait another entire year to bring him back to try again. Once Morals returned to his pen, he seemed satisfied he did not have to do anything he didn't want to, and shut his eyes to sleep. I thought, *Young man, you and I are going to have some schooling on manners in the coming year.*

When it was Ruby's time to show, she entered the show ring with a sweet, calm disposition and behaved perfectly in the ring, unlike her brother. She was also in an exceptionally large class and won third place. I was so proud of her. After the age classes were complete, the entrants were called into the ring for the "Best Headed" class. Ruby strutted in as if she were a queen, holding her beautiful head high. She was a strong contender for the Dorset breed. The judge walked up and down the line multiple times, carefully examining each entry. He stopped at me and

Ruby and reached out his hand for that special handshake. Ruby won the prestigious plaque for the "Best Headed" Dorset female in the country and her name was engraved on the beautiful wooden plaque. I returned home with Morals and Ruby, counting the days until we returned the following year.

I had reached my sixth year in Illinois and I continued to dedicate my life to my flock of Dorset sheep, giving it everything I had to become successful. Morals had grown and matured magnificently. He could only be shown for two years as a lamb, then the following year he could be shown as a yearling. After that, he would be retired to produce babies.

I had mated a few of my top females with Morals, and I was eagerly awaiting their lambs to arrive in the spring. There was so much riding on my new crop of lambs which would represent the third generation of my pedigree's bloodline. It is a well-known fact that the legacy of a true stud ram is validated if he sires a son who is better than himself. I used to believe that anyone could buy a champion, but true livestock breeders make their mark by creating bloodlines that advance the breed and leave a lasting legacy. It had always been of utmost importance to me to be known and respected as a successful breeder. I wanted to be remembered as such.

When the February birthing season arrived with its bitterly freezing weather, I was still being diligent with my night watches anticipating the arrival of new babies. Sure enough, on a frosty night at two in the morning, one of my best ewes, Katie, was in labor for the first time. She had been bred to Morals. Waiting to see the result was like waiting to open presents on Christmas morning! Katie was in labor for a few hours. I watched her closely as she pawed around the straw trying to make herself comfortable. She was lying down, grinding her teeth, getting up constantly, circling, looking behind her at the ground as if to say, "Is it out yet?" If only it was that easy! Finally, after some serious pushing with her legs outstretched, I could see the tips of hooves peeking out. Katie pushed and pushed, and when I decided she needed some help, I put on my delivery sleeves and carefully kneeled to assist her. I spoke gently to her as I softly stroked her face. She blinked her eyes at me with a look of trust. "Everything is going to be okay, Katie," I assured her. The lamb was in the correct position, and as I felt around, I could tell it was a huge lamb. After much patience and help from Katie pushing for several minutes, I pulled the lamb out and down carefully and gently. I gasped, "Oh my gosh" at how large the ram lamb was. He was not breathing so I held him up high by his rear legs as the mucous ran out of his nose, I wiped it clean and kept rubbing him briskly. In less than a minute, he was breathing freely on his own. I gently positioned him in front of Katie's face so she could see and care for her first lamb. Katie was overjoyed with her new baby lamb as she softly murmured to him, licking him dry.

My new ram lamb weighed in at twenty-one pounds. I was thrilled to witness the birth of the first baby lamb being born out of Morals. He was a masterpiece, and that is exactly what I named him. I stayed with Katie until I felt comfortable that Masterpiece was on his way to a solid start. I returned to the house to get a couple of hours of sleep before leaving for work As I exited the barn, I looked to the sky and thanked God for his blessing.

As the weeks passed, more baby lambs which had been sired by Morals were born. Each of them exhibited superb breed type and conformation, adorned with stunningly beautiful heads. I was in my glory, witnessing all the blessings arriving at my little farm. As the warm months of spring approached, I was feeling overjoyed with my new lambs showing much promise. Masterpiece was the shining gem in the group and Katie was the best mother to him. He was the leader of all the other baby lambs. They would run races outside in their pasture each day while their mothers were enjoying their meals. Masterpiece was always in the lead and wherever he went, the others followed, running as fast as their little legs could take them. They bounced and sprung about on all four legs at once as if they were made of springs. Occasionally they would throw out their rear legs like a bucking bull releasing energy and fun. They ran large circles around the pasture until their pink tongues hung out from exhaustion. That was always a positive sign that the baby lambs were feeling healthy and happy. Masterpiece won every race!

I registered Morals in the upcoming state fair to gauge his performance against others his age, now as Yearlings. He had outgrown his behavior issues and no longer acted like a spoiled teenager. We confidently walked into the show ring to line up beside approximately ten other rams all vying for the win. Morals behaved perfectly. I was proud of the way he looked compared to the others and thought he could do well in his class. As the judge examined each one as they walked in large circles, he chose Morals as the fifth-place winner. I was disappointed, but I had to keep in mind that each judge had their own opinion regarding their likes and dislikes in livestock. It can sometimes be fickle, but it is a part of competing. My faith and belief in Morals never weakened.

CHAPTER 41
Summit Achievement

The largest purebred livestock event in the world was once again held in Louisville. As usual, thousands of spectators traveled to the annual event from all over the world. Breeders, owners of all species, livestock magazine promoters, hundreds of agricultural industry leaders, breed representatives, and dignitaries from many countries came to compare their livestock to ours here in the United States. There was much to see and do as the collegiate livestock judging teams came to compete for national titles, and at the national rodeo final which was held during that time.

Morals and Masterpiece were now entered in the keenest of competitions. For many livestock showmen, it is a lifetime goal to gain the skills along with the quality of livestock to compete in that elite ring. If an entrant is ever lucky enough to step foot on the "sacred green shavings," it is a spiritual experience. Morals' class went first, and as I watched, I was clinching my hands together so tightly they were white. Among the other participants, he stood tall and majestic, alongside the rams he had competed with in August at the state fair. The judge carefully examined each entrant, running his hand down their backs to determine how long and straight they were. He felt their muscle expression in their rear quarters, and even looked at their teeth to verify their age and soundness. He requested that all the rams walk in a wide circle around the show ring, to determine how freely they flexed their legs as they walked for this is an important function in sheep. They must be sound and flexible while taking long, smooth strides while keeping their backs level as they move as it is important to exhibit a fluid movement, giving an overall impression of power, symmetry, and balance.

They must appear as a strong functional individual who would make a significant contribution to the sheep industry breeding programs. Finally, they had to have the look of a champion. The judge started selecting his bottom places first. As a showman, you do not want that first "finger point," you want the last one! He had already pulled out over ten sheep to place at the bottom of the class. Morals and two other rams were still on the side view. The pressure and anticipation were real. I said to myself, *Morals, please behave yourself.* The judge pointed to the third-place sheep. I felt like the moment was frozen in time when the judge gave a finger point to the second-place finisher. The final finger point went to Morals!! He was the class winner and was awarded the Mint Julip Silver Cup. The judge spoke very highly of Morals' attributes. He praised his eye appeal, style, size, substance, and balance, along with his robust constitution. As he spoke, Morals stood perfectly stately as if he was proudly soaking in all the compliments.

Morals had qualified to return to the show ring two hours later for the chance to earn the national title. My day had already been successful, and I was pleased with how my sheep had performed. The championship competition was broken down into two divisions. The first and second-place winners in the older age groups vied for the senior champion title. The younger aged group, under a year old, vied for junior champion honors. As we prepared for the next competition, Masterpiece was ready for his debut. He looked powerful in the lineup, and I was proud of how well he was representing my program. After thirty minutes of the judge walking up and down the line, examining each one thoroughly, he pointed to Masterpiece as the class winner, where he also won the Mint Julip Silver Cup award! It was difficult to find adequate words to describe the emotions I felt knowing that Masterpiece had qualified to return to the ring for the Junior Champion title.

When it was Morals' time to return to the ring, he stood poised for another examination by the judge against the other senior-level class winners. Walking around the ring several times deciding who the winner would be, the judge then returned to his microphone. He began to address the crowd sitting in the stands anxiously awaiting his results. He spoke highly of everyone in front of him, complimenting them for making their way through the competition. He slid the microphone back into its place, walked around the circle of competitors one final time, then pointed his finger to Morals as the Senior Champion ram!

Masterpiece was up next, competing for the Junior Champion title. Following the same routine as before, the judge carefully examined each sheep one last time. He extended his hand as the final handshake for Masterpiece being selected as winning the Junior Champion Ram title. Euphoria ran through my body as I marveled at the accomplishment that had just happened. I was the breeder of the best two Dorset rams in both age divisions!

To my knowledge, that was the first time in the history of that competition that a father/son combination was standing head-to-toe in the national championship ring at the same time. It was truly a moment in time that may not be duplicated, ever again. I stood, with my head held high, among breeders who I admired. They had some of the most magnificent quality sheep and were working with budgets and resources far beyond my reach. In spite of that difference, I had somehow clawed my way to the top to reach my heart's desire as a breeder of superior Dorsets.

Failure was never an option for me. I needed to prove to myself that I could do what I had just accomplished and exceed the expectations of others. I thought back to that discouraging and heartbreaking moment that occurred over thirty years earlier. The time when my father screamed at me saying, "You'll never be anything and you'll never raise a sheep without me." As I stood in the moment, taking in the events of the day, the adrenaline was shooting throughout my body, making me feel weak and drained. I had a private conversation with God, sending up prayers of thanksgiving from deep within my soul.

Morals was then awarded the Gold Medal for the day as he was crowned the National Champion Dorset Ram. Masterpiece was awarded the Junior National Champion Ram. Endless tears of joy slipped down my cheeks, to my neck, then onto my chest. I watched the show officials lay the prestigious dark purple felt champion banners with gold tassels adorned with bright gold letters "National Champion Dorset Ram" along with long streamed shiny purple rosettes over their backs. The banner represented that my sheep were considered royalty of their species.

Being validated was something I had sought my entire life, and that is what that moment presented to me. A lifelong dream was achieved and the feeling was indescribable. I reflected on all the difficulties I encountered that led to that point; the many devastating losses, disappointments, and setbacks remembering hearing some people years earlier whispering behind my back "She doesn't have a chance." At the time, I was not sure if I could ever overcome them. I learned how to dig myself out of the dark while turning losses into lessons and always gave it my best. I have never regretted any of the sacrifices I made along the way to become a good shepherd. Using my life's journey as an example of pure grit, determination and resilience, my goal now is to use my experiences to inspire others to "Never Give Up."

"Your journey is not the same as mine, and my journey is not yours, but if we meet on a certain path, may we encourage each other." – Author unknown

CHAPTER 42

The Best is Yet to Come

Five months after the overwhelming success at the nationals, a ram lamb that I also delivered on my farm was entered into the national show and sale to be sold at a public auction. He was beautiful in his breed type and conformation, just like his father, Morals. He brought stellar credentials as a future stud ram to the sale block. When coming into the sales, a lot depends on what other breeders need for their genetic improvements. There is also a lot of consideration concerning how the economy affects the livestock world. And most of all, if other breeders respect the bloodlines you have created. Most show sheep, on average, will sell for $500 to $2000.

As the first son of Morals walked into the sale block, whispers could be heard from the sidelines, "That is Morals' son." History was made that day. He sold for $20,000, holding the record for the third highest-selling Dorset ram of all time. A few months later I was honored that my name was submitted to the Continental Dorset Club (the national registrar) to be nominated into the Dorset Hall of Fame. For the rest of my time here on earth, I will honor what I feel is my responsibility to be God's shepherd to the beloved creatures known as sheep, whom I deeply cherish.

It has been my divine assignment to share with the world the heart of a good shepherd, for a good shepherd has a loving nature towards those entrusted to its care and does whatever it takes to protect the flock. As my life has unfolded, even throughout the toughest of times, my faith has remained. I have learned that even through the darkest of times, there is always a light to be found. Learning to appreciate the bright moments that have been sprinkled throughout my life and to always keep faith and hope alive is a message that I bring to the world. My prayer is that the adversity I have faced and overcome in my life encourages others to NEVER GIVE UP! My life is a true testimony of how faith, dedication, and resilience can lead to a life of overcoming adversity with grace.

I pray you do not become weary in well-doing. Know that in due season, you will reap a harvest of blessings and rewards you never dreamed possible. Never give up, and no matter what you do, never stop dreaming.

MY PARENTS NEVER CONSIDERED ME A PROFESSIONAL SHEPHERD.

However, I AM a shepherdess, beaten but never broken, and the best is yet to come.

About The Author

Debby Jo Holmquist is a true shepherdess. As soon as she could walk, her first destination was the sheep barn. She has spent her entire life amongst thousands of sheep, breeding, raising, and competitively showing her own registered Polled Dorset sheep for the past sixty years.

Of her many accomplishments, she has earned multiple National Championships throughout the United States and Canada along with being presented with many "Top Shepherd" awards. She was selected as an honorary Sheep Queen at the Canadian National Sheep "Sale of Stars" in Toronto, Canada at sixteen years old. One sheep she raised currently holds the record for the third highest-selling Dorset ram in the 126-year history of the breed.

Deb is a nationally certified Polled Dorset sheep judge and has served as a professional judge from coast to coast in North America and Canada, including the largest livestock show in the world, the North American International Livestock Exposition in Louisville, Kentucky four times.

Deb has recently been nominated into the Continental Dorset Club Hall of Fame.

She has endlessly volunteered hundreds of hours to young 4-H sheep members educating them on their sheep projects while empowering them to embrace their goals and dreams of one day becoming a top shepherd. She has even donated some of her show sheep to youngsters in need who had the dream, but not the means, to watch them fulfill their ambitions and win large championships.

Deb currently lives in Illinois, surrounded by her beloved Dorset sheep who continue to compete nationally. She has a deep love and understanding for all livestock. In her spare time, she enjoys landscaping flower gardens, mowing lawns, flower arranging, Large Pike fishing in Canada and playing with her beloved cats.

Debby Jo can be contacted at:
Debby Jo Holmquist
Show Girlz Sheep Company
1857 Ferrel Street
Paris, Illinois 61944 U.S.A.
Email: djoholmquist@gmail.com
Facebook: Debby Jo Holmquist,Author or Debby Jo Houle

www.ingramcontent.com/pod-product-compliance
Lightning Source LLC
Chambersburg PA
CBHW020448130626
46549CB00001B/346